AS Law for AQA

Jimmy O'Riordan

Heinemann Educational Publishers
Halley Court, Jordan Hill, Oxford OX2 8EJ
Part of Harcourt Education

Heinemann is the registered trademark of Harcourt Education Limited

Text © Jimmy O'Riordan 2002
Complete work © Harcourt Education Limited

First published in 2002

06 05
10 9 8 7 6 5

British Library Cataloguing in Publication Data
A catalogue record for this book is available from the British Library

10-digit ISBN: 0 435551 60 4
13-digit ISBN: 978 0 435551 60 5

Typeset by J&L Composition Ltd, Filey, North Yorkshire.
Illustrated by Simon Smith
Printed and bound in Great Britain by Scotprint, East Lothian

Cover photograph by: Photodisc

Tel: 01865 888058 www.heinemann.co.uk

Contents

Introduction

This book has been written specifically for the AQA AS law syllabus. The book uses key terms, summaries, short questions, spider graphs and examination tips. The book follows the AQA syllabus precisely so that you can plan your work. I have listened carefully to numerous AS law students who found many law books too detailed for their needs. I have therefore written this book with short sections, clear sentences and easy-to-read diagrams so that you understand the most important points. Each unit has revision questions to test what you have covered and exam questions with suggested answers to help you achieve higher grades.

Law is a fascinating subject which is contantly changing. I have therefore included suggestions for activities, visits, websites and newspaper readings. You can use these sources to support the key ideas covered in this book. Although I have listed many web addresses in the text, websites are constantly changing. Before you tackle a Web Activity, ask your teacher to suggest the most appropriate website, to make sure that you get the most up-to-date information.

Many thanks to my wonderful wife Catherine, who looked after our two energetic toddlers Alexander and Elizabeth, so that I could get on with writing this book. I would also like to thank all the students, teachers and librarians at High Pavement 6th Form College, Nottingham, for their advice, comments and contributions particularly Peter Welsby, Laura Burns, Kim Flower, Jane Parker and Kerry Piggott. Finally, thanks are due to Nigel Kelly, Caroline Pratt, Liz Tyler, Stephani Havard and Anne Forbes at Heinemann for their excellent support and guidance.

Jimmy O'Riordan
June 2002

Module 1 Law Making

Law makers

Unit 1

Sources of law and parliamentary supremacy

Key points

1 Statutory law
2 Common law/case law
3 Delegated legislation
4 Equity law
5 European law
6 Supremacy of Parliament

Why do I need to know about sources of law and the supremacy of Parliament?

For maximum marks you will need to have both knowledge of the law-making structures used in the English/European legal system and the ability to comment on the present state of affairs. You will also need an understanding of recent changes and proposals, such as those concerning the House of Commons and the House of Lords.

Sources of law

Understanding the key sources of law will give you an insight into the power relationships between various elements in the legal system. One of the most important issues to grasp is the development of the European and English legal systems since 1972, when the UK passed the **European Communities Act**, which became effective from 1 January 1973. Another limitation on the supremacy of Parliament is the **Human Rights Act 1998**. The topics looked at in this unit are explored more fully later in this module. For that reason it is important that you study this first unit carefully to get a good overview.

1 Statutory law

Law comes from a variety of sources as it is required to perform a variety of functions. Tensions may arise from time to time amongst the creators of law, but on the whole they know the benefits of having a harmonious legal system with all parts working together rather than competing. The first major source of law is *statutory law*.

Statutory law is law made by Parliament. It is passed using an Act of Parliament. The draft Act of Parliament is called a *bill*. A number of processes must be carried out in a variety of places before a law is finally passed.

1 **The House of Commons:** The House of Commons contains Members of Parliament voted into their jobs by ordinary people. Members of Parliament are there to represent the voters. A bill is presented to the House of Commons and goes through a number of stages before going to the House of Lords.

2 **The House of Lords:** Members of the House of Lords comment on and sometimes revise legislation which comes to them from the House of Commons. Some members are chosen by the Prime Minister, some inherit their jobs and soon some will be voted for by the people. After they have finished work on the legislation, it is passed to the Queen.

3 **The Queen:** In our present system the Queen must sign every law before it is finally passed. This is known as Royal Assent. It is a symbolic role. Since 1961 she does not even have the opportunity to read the legislation given to her by the Parliament. The Queen is not voted for by the people.

Parliament is the most important source of domestic legislation. It takes priority over other sources of domestic legislation since it has the backing of the people through the elected House of Commons. Parliament also has the power to cancel law (repeal). If it conflicts with European law, however, it is European law that takes priority. European law has **supremacy** when there is a clash.

Revision card activity

On an index card, list the key bodies responsible for passing statutory law.

Passage of legislation – Commons to Lords

Jargon buster

- A **statute** is another name for an Act of Parliament.

- **The Crown** is a term used to describe the government or the state when it has a Queen or King (monarch) at its head.

- **Supremacy** means having the highest status or power. If an organization has supremacy, its orders must be obeyed and its laws followed.

2   Common law/case law

Another extremely important source of law comes from decisions made by judges. This is known as *common* or *case law*. If a senior judge makes a decision on a case it is used in later similar cases. It becomes in effect a law. This process is known as ***judicial*** *precedent*.

Jargon buster

Judicial refers to the decisions and activities of judges. You will see this word used a great deal throughout your study of law.

Examination tip

You should try to read law cases covered in reputable newspapers such as *The Times*. It will help you understand the process of judicial decision-making.

3 Delegated legislation

When Parliament allows others to make law it is known as *delegated legislation*. This is an important source of law covering a vast range of issues and many different bodies. Local councils use delegated legislation. They are like mini local parliaments and need to pass laws regulating, for example, skateboarding, dogs in parks, parked cars and drunken behaviour in public places. They are trusted to pass local laws called by-laws. By-laws are local laws for local people. If there is a problem, then the government or relevant government department will normally look into it. Other forms of delegated legislation include *statutory instruments* passed by government departments and *Orders in Council*, which are laws passed when there is a national emergency.

Jargon buster

Delegation means passing authority, but not responsibility, downwards. If anything goes wrong, Parliament must still accept responsibility.

4 Equity law

In the past, when common law could not provide an opportunity for justice, claimants or defendants may have turned to the King's Chancellors for a solution. These important legal and political figures worked in the Court of Chancery from the thirteenth to the nineteenth century. The rulings of these Chancellors became law. Their job was to support common law when it appeared weak, rigid or ineffective. Even today, an important part of the High Court is known as the Chancery Division. These days the rulings of the Chancery Division of the High Court may also produce law through the process of judicial precedent.

Examination tip

Examiners are impressed with students who quote relevant Acts of Parliament or cases to support their line of argument.

5 European law

One of the most significant developments to affect the English legal system for hundreds of years was the passing of the **European Communities Act 1972** which came into force from January 1973. This joined the UK to the European Union and connected the English legal system to the European legal system. Europe is now an important and increasing source of new law.

Revision card activity

Identify the key creators of law in the English legal system.

European Law

6 Supremacy of Parliament

The United Kingdom belongs to an important economic and social organization called the European Union (EU). The EU has fifteen member states and its own legal system, to which we also belong. One of the pressing issues which had to be resolved by the EU was what would happen if national law in a member state conflicted with a law passed by the European Union. Which would take priority? Which system was supreme? An important groundbreaking case, *Factortame Ltd v Secretary of State (1989)*, confirmed that where there was a conflict between English law and European law, European law was supreme.

Revision card activity

Make notes on the importance of the EU and its impact on the English legal system.

Quick question

What would happen if individual members of the European Union adopted their own laws even when there was a European law?

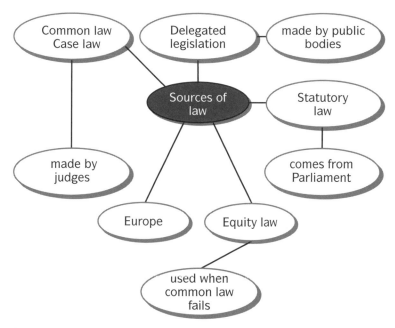

Sources of law

Group activity

List the creators of law in order of priority. Give reasons for your choices.

Examination tip

Questions on whether English or European law has supremacy are popular with examiners.

Revision checklist

1 Statutory law is created by Parliament.

2 A draft Act of Parliament is called a bill.

3 The House of Commons is voted into power by the people and passes laws which represent the interests of the country.

4 The House of Lords is a partly unelected element in the parliamentary system but has the right to comment on and amend legislation.

5 The Queen has to sign all legislation before it becomes law. This is known as Royal Assent. It is a symbolic activity.

6 Common law or case law is produced by the decisions of judges. The process is known as *judicial precedent*.

7 Delegated legislation occurs when Parliament allows responsible organizations such as local councils to pass laws affecting local people.

8 Equity law was produced by the King's Chancellor when common law was not up to the job.

9 European law is now an important source of law in the UK.

10 If there is a conflict between a law passed in the UK and one passed in Europe, then European law takes priority. European law is supreme.

Quick revision questions

1 What is a bill?

2 Who creates statutes?

3 Where does statutory legislation go to be passed?

4 What is Royal Assent?

5 What does supremacy mean?

6 Who creates common law?

7 What is a by-law?

8 Why did equity law come into being?

9 What did the **European Communities Act 1972** do?

10 Why was the *Factortame Ltd v Secretary of State (1989)* case so important?

Exam questions

1 Describe the main sources of English law. (15 marks)

2 Which source of law is most important? (15 marks)

Exam answer guide

1 Main sources of law used in the English legal system include:

✓ Statutory law created by Parliament

✓ Common law/case law created by judges' decisions

✓ Delegated legislation created by public bodies with the permission of Parliament

✓ Equity law was created by the King's Chancellor

✓ European law created by the institutions of the European Union.

2 This depends on the circumstances, but in general statutory law is probably the most important for most situations since it is backed by the votes of the electorate. European law is supreme when it comes to a conflict with English law. Common law and delegated legislation are important for the smooth running of the legal system. Parliament would not have time to examine each case or pass each local by-law. Equity law is possibly now the least important.

The formal legislative process

Key points

1. Main institutions in the system
2. Public bills
3. Private bills
4. Private Member's Bills
5. Stages in the progress of a bill

Why do I need to know about the formal legislative process?

Formal domestic legislation refers to law passed in our own parliamentary system. Many of the laws that we are familiar with on a day-to-day basis have been generated from the House of Commons and House of Lords. In the last unit we mentioned the growing importance of European law, but English law is still the backbone of our present system. The vast majority of cases heard in court use English legislation as their core. As a result you will be asked examination questions on the way that law is passed in the parliamentary system. To understand fully the process of producing legislation you

Domestic legislation

need to know the main institutions in the legislative system and the part played by each. Later in this module you will look at ways of producing law other than the parliamentary method.

1   Main institutions in the system

Most people over the age of 18 have the right to vote for someone who will represent their views in Parliament. The person who does this job is called their *Member of Parliament (MP)*. There are 659 MPs in the House of Commons who aim to represent the views of the electorate (the people who elect MPs). The power given to MPs is used to produce formal legislation through the Houses of Parliament. There are a number of elements and processes which you will need to understand.

Political parties

The vast majority of MPs belong to political parties. They might be members of the Labour Party, the Conservative Party or the Liberal Democratic Party. The political parties have different views about which laws should be passed and how the country should be run. The party with the most MPs normally has its way over what happens in Parliament. Tony Blair, the leader of the Labour Party, has significantly more MPs at present than any other party. Therefore the Labour Party normally wins any votes in the House of Commons over what laws should be passed. Another benefit of leading the party with the most MPs is that you are made Prime Minister.

The Cabinet

The Prime Minister selects the Cabinet as his or her working team. Members of the Cabinet are normally MPs. The Cabinet is a group of the most senior and powerful elected Members of Parliament in the winning political party. It proposes legislation by putting forward a document called a *bill*. A bill is like a draft copy of an Act of Parliament and it is used for discussion purposes. It must go through a number of stages before it becomes law. If the Prime Minister and the Cabinet support the bill, then it has an excellent chance of becoming law. We will look at this process during this unit.

The Government

The Government is formed by the party which wins the most seats in the general election. The Queen invites the leader of the party who has the most MPs to form the new Government, i.e. to take charge of the country and select the Cabinet. The Prime Minister now forms 'Her Majesty's Government'. In theory the Queen could refuse to make the leader of the largest party the Prime Minister. In reality this never happens.

The House of Lords

In addition to the elected House of Commons there is another element to the parliamentary system called the House of Lords. In theory the Lords have a say in what legislation is passed and what is not. Members of the House of Lords see themselves as a revising chamber. This means looking once again at legislation and improving parts which may have been missed in drafting or in the House of Commons. The House of Lords is seen as a balance to the power of the House of Commons.

The present Government has introduced a number of changes to reduce the power of the House of Lords and modernize its procedures. The numbers in the House of Lords have been reduced, but it still remains a powerful part of the parliamentary system. However, the **Parliament Acts 1911** and **1949** allow the House of Commons to pass legislation without the consent of the House of Lords.

The Crown

The power of the monarch in times past is still seen today in the theoretical power of the Crown to pass or reject legislation. The monarch has to give permission for any Act of Parliament to be put into force. This is known as Royal Assent. In the real world, however, the Queen would never refuse – it is a mere formality. Just as the English legal system would never really want a showdown with the European Court of Justice, the Queen would gain nothing by flexing her muscles with the Houses of Parliament. A delicate balance of power exists in the system. The last time a monarch refused a piece of legislation which had been passed by the Houses of Parliament was in 1707.

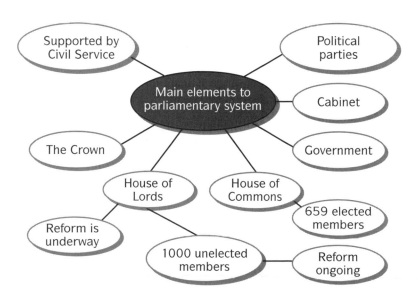

Main elements of the parliamentary system

Royal assent

Did you know?

Certain people cannot vote. They include:

- people who are mentally incapable
- convicted prisoners in jail
- the Queen
- people who have not registered to vote.

Group activity

What are the pros and cons of involving the House of Commons, the House of Lords and the Queen when passing legislation?

Examination tip

Read quality newspapers so that you are up to date with developments in the issues concerning Parliament.

2 Public bills

The Government introduces most bills which come before the Houses of Parliament. These bills attempt to meet the promises made by the winning party during the election campaign. If the Government has a big majority of MPs, these bills will almost certainly be passed and become law. Government bills are known as public bills.

Jargon buster

During the election campaign each political party publishes a list of its promises and commitments. The booklet containing these is called the **manifesto**.

3 Private bills

Private bills are proposed by particular institutions or individuals. A local authority might want to build a new road network or a modern tram system and may use a private bill. In the past railways were established by the use of bills. More recently a plan to change the ownership of the John Lewis shops failed because those involved did not have the resources to push a bill through Parliament.

Examination tip

Use revision cards to break complex ideas into simpler ones.

4 Private Member's Bills

A small amount of parliamentary time is spent discussing Private Member's Bills. These are bills put forward by individual MPs. The bills reflect issues that are close to the hearts of the MPs putting them forward. Most Private Member's Bills that are successful have Government support. The majority of the bills put forward are non-controversial, but there have been some notable exceptions.

1   The abolition of the death penalty came about from a Private Member's Bill which led to **The Murder (abolition of death penalty) Act 1965**.

2   **Abortion Act 1967**: an MP called David Steele put this Private Member's Bill forward. The issues divided many people and are still the subject of controversy in some circles.

3   A bill to ban foxhunting has still not seen the light of day. Powerful pressure groups have mobilized against the passing of this legislation and the Government is still considering its position.

Quick question

What is the difference between a public and a private bill?

Revision card activity

Note the various places legislation comes from.

5 | Stages in the progress of a bill

A bill is the name for a *draft Act of Parliament*. Bills come in two main forms, public and private. They can start in the House of Commons or the House of Lords (except for all important finance bills which must start in the House of Commons). If the bill is to become law it must go through a number of stages, each one improving the quality of the legislation and allowing input from relevant contributors.

1 A Green Paper is issued to act as a focus for discussion. When the Government wishes to hear from those interested in an area of law that it is planning to change, a Green Paper is issued. This is the first stage in the process of public consultation. Contributions from those interested are sent to the relevant Government department. The Government then has the opportunity to consider the points of view both of those who support and of those who oppose the potential changes. Early consultation is seen as producing better legislation and allowing those who object to have their say. The Government may revise the ideas it first considered based on the feedback it receives.

2 A White Paper is issued which builds on the consultation carried out in the Green Paper. The Government's proposals are firmer at this stage. Any relevant contributions it has received from its Green Paper process are incorporated into the White Paper. The White Paper offers more focused debate on the developed proposals. Eventually a *bill* will be introduced to Parliament for its consideration which is based on the White Paper. It will have to go through several stages before it becomes a law.

3 The bill is put before the House of Commons for three readings, a Committee Stage and a Report Stage.

   a **First Reading** gives information about the name of the bill and its main intentions. A vote is taken in the house, usually verbally. If there are enough ayes (votes in support) the bill is carried forward to the next stage.

   b **Second Reading** is the main debate on the bill's proposals in the House of Commons. Members of Parliament have an opportunity to discuss and debate and test the bill's strengths and weaknesses. There is a vote at the end of the second reading which determines whether the bill goes further or not.

c **Committee Stage** involves a more detailed examination of the bill. A committee of the House of Commons which reflects the political strength of each of the main parties sits and goes through this process.

d **Report Stage** allows MPs the chance to debate any changes introduced at the Committee Stage. If there are no changes the Bill will go through to the Third Reading.

e **Third Reading** is the final stage of the bill's progress in the House that it started in. If it started in the House of Commons, MPs will now vote on whether to accept it or not. It is very unlikely to fail at this point since it has already been through a number of stages where any opposition could have been examined and dealt with. This stage is normally a formality.

4 If the bill started in the House of Commons it is now put before the House of Lords for the same process it went through in the Commons.

5 The Queen gives her Royal Assent. This is another formality. The Queen does not even have the text of the bill in front of her since the **Royal Assent Act 1961**.

6 The Act of Parliament is now law.

The House of Commons is the elected part of Parliament and therefore has the most power. If a bill goes to the House of Lords and there are problems with its passage, the House of Commons can overrule the Lords. The legislation used to do this is contained in the **Parliament Act 1911** and the **Parliament Act 1949**. The bill must be introduced to the House of Commons again and pass all stages again. This clearly slows down the process, and the Prime Minister and the Government do not look on it kindly. The House of Lords is now seen as a revising chamber and not there to oppose the democratically elected Government of the people.

Clearly this is a long and complicated process which has a great deal of scope for delay and confusion. Normally the whole process takes a number of months although, in times of national emergency, legislation can be passed within a couple of days. The Government often passes the job of drafting and passing legislation to others. This is known as *delegated legislation*.

Group activity

The Houses of Parliament can be visited. You can watch the proceedings from the public gallery and may even get a guided visit if Parliament is not sitting. If a visit is not possible, there is regular coverage on TV and even a cable channel for the very enthusiastic.

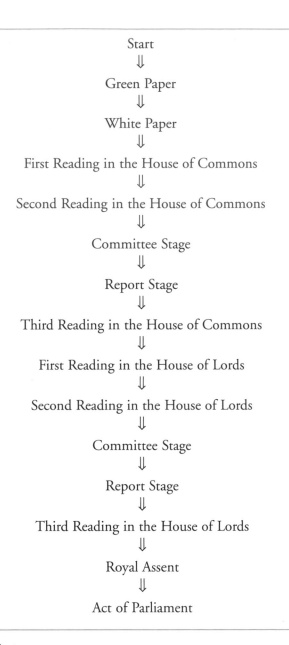

Start
⇓
Green Paper
⇓
White Paper
⇓
First Reading in the House of Commons
⇓
Second Reading in the House of Commons
⇓
Committee Stage
⇓
Report Stage
⇓
Third Reading in the House of Commons
⇓
First Reading in the House of Lords
⇓
Second Reading in the House of Lords
⇓
Committee Stage
⇓
Report Stage
⇓
Third Reading in the House of Lords
⇓
Royal Assent
⇓
Act of Parliament

The passage of legislation

Revision card activity

Using cards, list the key stages in the progress of a piece of legislation.

The Parliament Acts

Examination tips

- The highest marks will be given to students who can accurately describe and comment on processes such as the passage of legislation. Any diagrams you use must also be accompanied by a full explanation.

- Find some examples of delegated legislation to quote in your answers.

Mandate and manifesto

The content of parliamentary legislation is governed to a certain extent by what is promised in the manifesto of the winning party. The manifesto contains promises by political parties to the electorate before the election. When a particular party wins power it has the backing of the voters for its policies. This is known as their mandate. It is what gives the UK Government power to pass law. The only limitations on this power are conflict with the European Union, if law is passed in the same area, and the Human Rights Act 1998.

Revision checklist

1 Green Papers are used to start discussions on areas of law that Governments are planning to change.

2 Contributors to Green Papers send their ideas or objections to the relevant Government department.

3 White Papers are produced after all comments on the Green Paper have been received and reviewed. They are firmer proposals.

4 Public bills come from Government and cover major promises made in the manifesto. Private bills relate to individual institutions or local authorities.

5 Private Member's Bills are started by individual Members of Parliament. They express the concerns of those members and unless they are supported by the Government they rarely make it to the end of the process.

6 The main stages in the progress of legislation are: Green Paper, White Paper, First Reading, Second Reading, Committee Stage, Report Stage, Third Reading, passed to the other House of Parliament for the same process, signed by the Queen and then finally law.

7 A bill normally takes a great deal of time to get through all stages, but emergency legislation can be passed within a couple of days.

8 The House of Commons is elected by the people while the House of Lords contains some parliamentarians who have been given their jobs by politicians.

9 The **Parliament Acts of 1911** and **1949** allow the House of Commons to overrule the House of Lords if there is resistance to a bill.

10 If the **Parliament Act** is used, the legislation has to be reintroduced to the Commons in the next session of Parliament and pass all stages again.

Quick revision questions

1 What is the importance of a Green Paper?

2 What is a White Paper?

3 What is the difference between a Public Bill, a Private Bill and a Private Member's Bill?

4 Name a Private Member's Bill which has become law.

5 What happens during the First and Second Reading of a Bill?

6 What does the Committee Stage involve?

7 What does the Report Stage allow MPs to do?

8 Outline details of the Third Reading.

9 What role does the Queen play in the passing of legislation?

10 What do the **Parliament Acts** allow the House of Commons to do?

Exam questions

1 *a* Outline the key stages in the passing of an Act of Parliament. (10 marks)

 b How far does legislation reflect what the Government wishes? (20 marks)

Exam answer guide

1 *a* The key stages in the passing of an Act of Parliament are:

✓ Green Paper

✓ White Paper

✓ First Reading

✓ Second Reading

✓ Committee Stage

✓ Report Stage

✓ Third Reading

✓ Passed to other House of Parliament for repeat

✓ Queen gives assent

✓ Act is law.

 b The process of altering the bill probably starts with the Green Paper system which allows outside feedback on the Government's proposals. Opposition parties (and the Government's own backbenchers) may try to change legislation at Green Paper/White Paper Stage onwards. Committee Stage involving MPs from all main parties may add or take away from the bill. House of Lords may put amendments into legislation to change its flavour and even its direction. The Queen could refuse to sign the bill (but in reality would never do such a thing). All in all there are many opportunities to influence and change the provisions and nature of the bill as it goes on its travels.

Unit 3

Influences on Parliament

Why do I need to know about influences on Parliament?

Questions on influences on Parliament will expect you to understand the main official and unofficial sources of these pressures. Some are obvious, but some are subtle. The whole legal system is a mix of solid, predictable legislation and built-in flexibility for a society that is fast moving. You will need to understand where the pressure for change comes from and how the system can respond. Examples of recent cases and current issues will improve your marks.

Influences on Parliament

1 The Civil Service

The Civil Service is responsible for advising the Government and putting into place the paperwork to ensure that Government policies promised in the manifesto actually happen. The Civil Service prides itself on its non-political nature. It is not, however, a completely neutral organization. Senior civil servants, in particular, have great power within the parliamentary system. They advise ministers on issues of concern and are responsible for many of the ideas put forward for the minister to think about. Unlike politicians, they stay in their jobs for many, many years. Changes of Government do not affect them. This allows them to build up considerable expertise and power. They understand the 'system' much more thoroughly than most new ministers. They often 'use' the system for their own goals.

Senior civil servants can exert influence by deciding what is discussed at meetings and what information is provided and not provided to ministers. This gives them enormous scope for subtle influence on Parliament through Government departments and the ministers who run them.

Group activity

Examine the pros and cons of the contribution of the Civil Service to the creation of legislation.

2 The role of the Law Commission

The Law Commission is an advisory body set up in 1965. It researches areas of law that could benefit from reform and produces draft bills for passage through Parliament. It was part of the Government's plan to 'modernize' Britain. It is the only full-time, permanent, Government-funded organization that investigates and comments on law reform. English law is a combination of statute law and common law, some of which goes back a very long time. The Law Commission's job is to:

'keep under review all the law with a view to its systematic development.'

The work of law reform is ultimately the concern of Parliament, but the Law Commission provides useful research and ideas which contribute to debate on legal issues. The Commission consults widely on issues of concern and has five full-time officials who coordinate the information and put it into an effective vehicle for change. The Commission does not offer legal advice to individuals or organizations but is more concerned with wider legal issues. The Lord Chancellor's Department often refers areas it wants explored to the Law Commission.

The organization is made up of people from the legal profession. It includes a High Court Judge, a Queen's Counsel (QC), a solicitor, and two legal academics. The

Commission is also supported by a range of administrative staff, including Parliamentary Counsel who draft Government bills.

Work of the Law Commission

The Law Commission works on about 20 or 30 projects at any one time. A project will attempt to identify any defects in the current system and then look for possible solutions. It may possibly look at how foreign legal systems deal with similar issues.

In its first 25 years the Law Commission produced 100 reports, over 70 per cent of which resulted in legislation.

There are five key areas of concern for the Law Commission.

- The development and reform of law.

- Getting rid of outdated law (repealing obsolete law).

- The simplification of the law.

- Codifying the law (that is, putting it all in one place).

- Getting rid of laws which conflict with each other.

The Law Commission

Group activity

Can you think of any areas of law which might benefit from reform? Who would you ask for their opinions on the issue?

Revision card activities

- Using an index card, list the main figures in the Law Commission.

- Note the key areas of work of the Law Commission.

Examination tip

Start revision early. This allows time for ideas to mature and relationships in the syllabus to become clearer.

3 | Royal Commissions

When an area of law causes public concern, a Royal Commission is often set up. A Royal Commission is made up of a large cross-section of people. All have an interest in the issue explored, but most are not legally qualified.

The Commission undertakes research, interviews relevant parties, and then publishes a report. Parliament is under no obligation to act on the recommendations of a Royal Commission, even though the process may take many months or even years to complete and represent innovative and valuable contributions to the area under investigation.

Examples of Royal Commissions include:

- Royal Commission on Police Procedure in 1981, which had many of its recommendations incorporated into the **Police and Criminal Evidence Act 1984**

- Royal Commission on Civil Liability and Compensation in 1978, which investigated awards for medical care and social security benefits

- Royal Commission on Justices of the Peace in 1948, which was one of the first and most revealing investigations into the backgrounds of lay magistrates.

Web activity

Identify any current Royal Commissions and the reasons for their enquiries.

4 Public enquiries and other official bodies

Public enquiries

Public enquiries are often set up after high-profile disasters. They frequently lead to changes in the law to prevent a reoccurrence of the event. Recent public enquiries include:

- **Enquiry into the BSE crisis** – This looked at the possible reasons for the spread of the disease amongst cattle and then into humans in the form of new variant CJD.

- **Hillsborough enquiry** – This looked at the tragic events surrounding the deaths of football fans in the Hillsborough stadium in Sheffield.

- **Alder Hey Children's Hospital enquiry** – The scandal at Alder Hey Children's Hospital in Liverpool involved doctors keeping parts of dead children for research purposes, without informing the children's parents.

- **Paddington train crash enquiry** – The troubles on the railway system have caused a series of high-profile crashes which have killed passengers and crew. The enquiry looked not only at the events on the day but also at the factors behind the incident.

Public enquiries are designed to get behind the facts and provide information to stop the same circumstances arising again. They have no power to implement their proposals. This is for the Government to consider and respond.

Law Reform Committee

This is a small, part-time committee which focuses on specialized areas which need technical legal solutions. It was formed in 1952 and is still at times consulted by the Law Commission. The Lord Chancellor refers work to it occasionally. It is only involved with civil law.

The Criminal Law Revision Committee

This committee plays a similar role to the Law Reform Committee, but handles criminal law. The **Theft Acts** are its main area of success. As with the Law Reform Committee, this is a part-time group.

Group activity

Public enquiries are designed to get at the truth and stop similar disasters. What obstacles may prevent the implementation of recommendations?

Revision card activities

- Note the key public enquiries mentioned for use in your written work.

- Using cards, list and revise the work of the Law Commission, the Law Reform Committee and the Criminal Law Revision Committee.

Examination tip

Give examples of the work of the Law Commission, the Royal Commissions and other law reform bodies.

5 The influence of judges

Judges are keen not to tread on the toes of Parliament/Government. In fact, they often state that they are trying to uphold the position of the Parliament/Government rather than compete with it. They are, however, faced with the practical problems of their actions. What they decide will have implications for public policy and the actions of ordinary people, organizations and even Government departments and local authorities in the future.

Lord Radcliffe, a famous Law Lord of the 1960s, said: 'It is unacceptable that there should be two independent sources of law making at work at the same time'. This careful line is one present-day judges try to steer, although at times it is very difficult.

Examination tip

Develop each of your points fully to gain maximum credit. Do not try to cover too many points.

6 General public and the media

Sometimes it is difficult to know whether the media influence what the public think or the public influence what the media cover. Either way, the two forces are individually very powerful and together almost irresistible.

The general public

One of the main problems we have is trying to identify who the general public are. We live in a rich and varied society, and the concept of one 'general public' is complex. Opinion polls by political parties may indicate where the 'majority' of the public are on any one issue, and popular legislation may follow.

A case which involved individuals, the 'general public' and the media was the tragic case in 2001 of Sarah Payne. The parents of the murdered child have campaigned for a radical change in the law so paedophile offenders would be publicly named. The Home Office and the Police have reservations, but some change in the law looks likely. A national Sunday tabloid and several local newspapers around the country supported the bereaved parents by naming suspected offenders, with some very dangerous results. A paediatrician who spent his entire professional life caring for children's health had his house attacked by an ill-informed and angry mob. Parliament is sensitive to such strong vocal emotions and campaigns.

The media

We live in a world where media influence is very powerful. Some say that it can even decide the outcome of elections. The Government is clearly moved by focused media pressure such as that surrounding dangerous dogs, protection of children and even the way that judges give sentences to criminals. The case of Sarah Payne just mentioned is a good illustration of the power of newspapers and media to bring enormous pressure on Parliament. The entire electorate is subject to the messages of the media. The media have increasingly provided the agenda for much parliamentary debate and even legislation.

Examination tip

Always seek help from your teacher if you do not understand any concept. Law is difficult at times for all of us.

7 Pressure groups and lobbyists

Political pressure groups

Groups both inside and outside Parliament have political campaigns which they want supported by favourable legislation. MPs and those who have influence on Parliament are lobbied for their support. The topics are endless and range from the banning of landmines to the legalization of cannabis.

Professional lobbyists

The world of professional lobbyists started in the United States but is well and truly part of our system now. Specialists are hired by big businesses and organizations to put their points of view in the most effective way. The methods used are sometimes very questionable.

Environmental groups

Groups such as Greenpeace and Friends of the Earth have been extremely successful in raising the issue of environmental damage. They skilfully put their message to the public by using sophisticated publicity stunts which the media use as news. Legislation passed to date in the UK has been relatively weak, however. Forthcoming European legislation promises to be much more hard-hitting.

Civil rights groups

A number of high-profile groups focus on particular areas of the law to bring about change and improvement. For example, the campaigning group Liberty uses its resources to oppose or amend legislative changes that it believes may reduce our civil liberties and freedoms. Liberty has been in the forefront of pressures to bring about freedom of information laws and has bitterly opposed the ending of the 'right to silence' and changes planned for the curbing of right to trial by jury.

Penal reformers

Organizations such as The Howard League and the National Association for the Care and Rehabilitation of Offenders specialize in improving the prison system and its aftercare facilities through changes in legislation.

Race relations and bureaucratic reform

Clearly one of the most successful campaigns of recent years surrounded the tragic death of Stephen Lawrence, the black teenager from south-east London. The Macpherson Report investigated the murder and its investigation and made many recommendations for change. Some of these related to the way whole institutions discriminate against ethnic minorities. The term 'institutionalized racism' was used many times in the report.

Trade unions

Trade unions have had more influence since the election of a Labour Government. They now speak directly to the Prime Minister. Many MPs are sponsored by trade unions and will speak on topics affecting trade union members.

Other pressure groups

Other pressure groups include charities, churches, big businesses, farmers, scientists, welfare organizations, consumer groups and dedicated individuals.

Group activity

Try to arrange a visit to a trade union office or have a representative come into your school or college. This will help you to get an idea of the areas of law unions are interested in reforming.

Web activity

Look for Liberty's website on the Internet at www.liberty.org.uk. What are the group's current areas of focus?

Research activities

- Find out more about the legal campaigns run by major pressure groups. Greenpeace and Friends of the Earth have very efficient press offices you can contact. Also use the Internet and your local library.

- Try to find some pages from *Hansard*, the official record of the Houses of Parliament. The Internet would be a good place to start. Identify the various lines of argument taken by different speakers.

Influences on Parliament

Make sure you have the correct AQA AS law syllabus and tick off topics as you have revised them.

Revision checklist

1 The Civil Service often has a subtle influence on the direction of legislation.

2 The Law Commission is the only full-time, Government-funded body looking at the development of law.

3 The Law Commission's work involves: the development and reform of law, getting rid of outdated law (repealing obsolete law), the simplification of the law, and codifying the law (meaning putting it all in one place).

4 The Law Commission is staffed by a High Court Judge, a QC, a solicitor, and two legal academics.

5 The Law Commission works on 20–30 projects at the same time and has had a reasonable success rate in turning proposals into law.

6 The Lord Chancellor often asks the Law Commission to look at specific areas of law.

7 Pressure is placed on members of the Houses of Parliament by: political pressure groups, lobbyists, environmental groups, penal reformers, campaign groups, trade unions, the media and the general public.

8 Political lobbyists are professionals who try to persuade MPs of the virtue of their clients' cases.

9 Trade unions influence Parliament by sponsoring MPs.

10 Pressure groups attempt to target the general public using media coverage.

Quick revision questions

1 How does the Civil Service affect the passage of legislation?

2 What is the Law Commission's main aim?

3 Who sits on the Law Commission?

4 Name some recent Royal Commissions and Public Enquiries.

5 What do the Law Reform Committee and the Criminal Law Revision Committee do?

6 Does the Queen play a part in the development of law?

7 Why are judges careful when developing new law?

8 Name six pressure groups that influence Parliament.

9 What does a political lobbyist do?

10 How do trade unions exert influence on Parliament?

Exam questions

1 a Where do the main pressures for changes in the law come from? (10 marks)

   b Who should decide what laws are passed? (20 marks)

Exam answer guide

1 a Main pressures come from:

✓ MPs within Parliament

✓ Pressure groups and lobbyists

✓ Media sources

✓ General public

✓ Big businesses

✓ Churches and charities

✓ Welfare organizations

✓ Consumer groups

✓ Individuals and small groups.

   b Who should make laws is a complex question. Possible answers include:

✓ MPs who represent the general public

✓ Cabinet on behalf of the country

✓ Government departments

✓ Local authorities

✓ Any from part **a** are worth considering.

Drafting law is a complex business and the present system at least consults widely on all legislation to be passed so that the credit or blame can be shared out.

Unit 4 Delegated legislation

Why do I need to know about delegated legislation?

Questions on delegated legislation go to the heart of law making. Parliament cannot afford the time to pass legislation for all who need it, so some legislation is passed to responsible bodies such as local councils and large organizations such as the railways to create legislation for themselves. Questions will focus on how delegated legislation is created and how it is controlled. You will need to put arguments for and against the entire process of delegating power to organizations to pass law and give your opinion on this system.

Delegated legislation

1 Delegated legislation

Delegation means passing power downwards. In the English legal system this means passing power downwards from Parliament to organizations and bodies that need to pass laws for their own purposes. Delegated legislation has grown alongside the significant growth in the Welfare State since 1945. Although authority is passed downwards, any legislation passed is still ultimately the responsibility of Parliament.

2 Reasons for delegating legislative powers

Political parties struggle to achieve power, but there are good reasons why the party in office is keen to see others exercise it.

Organizations with delegated responsibility

The following bodies have been trusted with this authority:

- **Government departments**, such as the Home Office who want to introduce new laws curbing criminal behaviour, or the Benefits Agency introducing new types of benefit payments to clients.

- **Public organizations**, such as London Transport who want to launch new regulations such as a smoking ban on the underground network, or the railways who need to tighten security to prevent injuries.

- **Local authorities**, who may be introducing car-free city centres or banning alcohol in town centres.

Reasons for delegation

There are a number of reasons why Parliament is happy to allow these various organizations to consult, draft and introduce their own legislation.

- **Limited parliamentary time** – Parliament has a limited amount of time to pass legislation and the Government of the day chooses to push its own major legislation through Parliament. Each Government makes certain promises in its manifesto. If it is to retain its credibility, it needs to keep at least some of the promises it made before the election.

- **Local knowledge** – Parliament may feel that it is not the best institution to recognize and deal with the needs of local people. Politicians called Councillors are elected by local people to run local authorities. It is in the interests of Councillors to pass legislation known as by-laws to satisfy local needs, if they want to be re-elected.

- **Specialization** – Parliament contains MPs from a wealth of backgrounds. They cannot, however, be expert in everything. There are times when only the

Reasons for delegated legislation

professionals can do the job properly. The **1984 Social Security Act** brought complex changes in the payments of Income Support. Professionals in the Department of Social Security developed the legislation and reviewed its effectiveness.

- **Fast response** – Delegated legislation can often respond to changing needs more quickly than a full passage through the parliamentary system. Most bills take several months to go through the many stages needed, even when there is no opposition to them. Delegated legislation can be completed much more quickly. A new system for paying Income Support benefits came into force in 1987. There were to be no payments of Income Support to anyone under the age of 18. This caused great hardship to some unsupported younger people. Within a few days a new system of hardship payments came into force. This was an example of a very rapid response using delegated legislation to amend the law.

- **Future needs** – Drafting of legislation cannot always take into account the changes that may come about in the future. Delegated legislation can be used to amend legislation more quickly and more effectively.

3   The creation of delegated legislation

There are a number of methods used to produce delegated legislation.

Statutory Instruments

Government departments create Statutory Instruments, which are pieces of legislation that relate to the work of that department. At times, these are called ministerial regulations. The departments are given permission by a **Parent Act**. This gives guidance about how the new piece of legislation is to be written and processed. The Parent Act is also sometimes known as an *enabling act* because it enables the department to pass the legislation.

A Statutory Instrument (SI) may cover the changing of road signs by the Department of Transport or changes to safety law by the Health and Safety Executive. SIs give departments immense freedom to change the law and are used about 3000 times per year. There are two ways for a Statutory Instrument to become law.

- **Negative resolution procedure** – After the SI is written it is shown to Parliament. It is now technically a piece of law. If no one objects to its contents within 40 days, then it becomes permanent. If there are objections then the SI must be debated in the House of Commons, the House of Lords or in a Standing Committee. It may be passed or it may be rejected.

- **Affirmative resolution procedure** – If the SI is controversial, then Parliament may put an instruction in the Parent Act that the issue has to be debated and voted on before it becomes law.

By-laws

Nottingham City Council, along with many other **local authorities** in the country, is enforcing a car ban in the City Centre area. Power to do this comes in the form of a piece of delegated legislation known as a by-law.

Other public bodies such as the railways can create and enforce by-laws. These are often about not buying tickets, drunken behaviour or smoking.

Examination tip

Use examples of local by-laws to illustrate delegated legislation.

Orders in Council

Delegated legislation involves bodies below Parliament passing legislation for one reason or another. Orders in Council are laws passed in an emergency when Parliament is not sitting. This Council consists of the Queen and the **Privy Council**.

Until recently, it was difficult to think of an occasion when Parliament would be so incapacitated that the Queen and the Lord Chancellor were making delegated legislation. The bombing of the World Trade Centre in September 2001 gave a chilling insight into the possibility of this happening. There were rumours that the Houses of Parliament were on the list of buildings to be attacked. If this nightmare had come true, Orders in Council may have been used as a last resort. The power of Orders in Council comes from the **Emergency Powers Act 1920**.

Orders in Council have, however, been made to cover such incidents as:

- the foot and mouth crisis, which demanded immediate action to limit the spread of the disease across the UK

- the fuel protests, when lorry drivers and farmers blockaded oil depots to prevent vital supplies reaching customers as a protest against higher fuel prices.

Parliament was not sitting at key points during these times, and people at the top took decisions quickly. Debate in Parliament followed some time later.

Jargon buster

- A **local authority** is another name for a local council.

- The **Privy Council** is made up of senior politicians, past and present, and other distinguished people. The **Judicial Committee of the Privy Council** consists of judges, including the Lord Chancellor, and is a Court of Appeal for some cases.

Research activity

Many by-laws are very publicly displayed, although most of the time we probably do not even see them. Over the next week, see how many by-laws you can identify. Buses, trains and streets in town are rich pickings.

Examination tip

Give examples of each of the main types of delegated legislation when you answer questions on this topic.

4 Control and supervision of delegated legislation

Giving power away does not mean that responsibility is given away. At the end of the day Government takes the blame if things go wrong. It is therefore keen to monitor, and to curb if it proves necessary. There are a number of ways that delegated legislation is controlled.

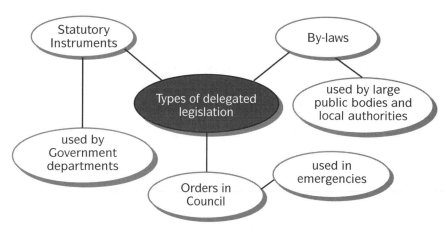

Types of delegated legislation

Scrutiny Committee

The Joint Select Committee on Statutory Instruments is responsible for checking SIs and letting Parliament know of any problems. It is also known as the Scrutiny Committee (*scrutiny* means looking at something in close detail). Possible reasons for informing Parliament of any problems with SIs include an organization going beyond its powers (this is known as *ultra vires*), imposing a tax (which it is not allowed to do), producing unclear legislation or producing retrospective legislation (backdating an offence).

Judicial review

All delegated legislation can be judicially reviewed. This means taking the case to the Queen's Bench Division of the High Court and getting a High Court Judge to decide whether the new legislation is in order or not. The most common reason for objecting to delegated legislation is that the organization acted beyond its powers (*ultra vires*).

Parent Act

The Parent Act which gave power in the first place should be carefully drafted to make sure that defects and problems are reduced to the minimum. Ministerial approval is used to support the monitoring of delegated legislation.

Scrutiny

5 | Evaluation of delegated legislation

What are the overall benefits and drawbacks of delegated legislation?

The advantages include:

- Delegated legislation saves time in Parliament that can be used for 'more important' pieces of legislation. Manifesto promises are a priority.

- MPs are not experts in all fields, so delegation allows the use of expert civil servants or other professionals to explore the details.

- Delegated legislation allows a quick response to changing circumstances or mistakes.

- Delegated legislation is scrutinized by committees who have time to look into the details of the legislation.

The disadvantages include:

- Delegated legislation may be undemocratic: unelected civil servants in powerful Government departments draft the law.

- The public may find it difficult to keep up with the volume of change.

- Delegation may give some opportunity for avoiding blame if things go wrong.

With our complex society it would probably now be impossible to do without delegated legislation. The only thing we can hope for is that it is properly monitored and controlled.

Revision checklist

1 Delegated legislation saves time in Parliament that can be used for 'more important' pieces of legislation.
2 Parent Act/enabling act gives guidance on what can be put into a particular piece of delegated legislation.
3 MPs are not experts in all fields so delegation allows the use of expert civil servants or other professionals to explore the details.
4 Delegated legislation allows a quick response to changing circumstances or mistakes.
5 Delegated legislation is scrutinized by committees who have time to look into the details of the legislation.
6 Delegated legislation may be called undemocratic. Unelected civil servants in powerful Government departments draft the law.
7 Public may find it difficult to keep up with the volume of change.
8 Delegation may give some opportunity for avoiding blame if things go wrong.
9 Main forms of delegated legislation are Orders in Council, Statutory Instruments and by-laws.
10 Delegated legislation is covered by judicial review.

Quick revision questions

1 Who are the main players in Orders in Council?

2 Who produces Statutory Instruments?

3 What are by-laws?

4 Who uses by-laws?

5 What does the Scrutiny Committee do?

6 What are the main reasons for finding a problem with a piece of delegated legislation?

7 When are judicial reviews normally used with delegated legislation?

8 Who are the main users of delegated legislation?

9 Why is delegated legislation such a good idea?

10 What is a Parent Act?

Exam questions

1 *a* Who are the main users of delegated legislation? (10 marks)

 b Should all legislation go through elected bodies? (20 marks)

Exam answer guide

1 *a* Main users include:

 ✓ Government departments

 ✓ Local authorities

 ✓ Public bodies.

 Give examples of the types of use delegated legislation is put to.

 b Although Government departments are not directly elected, the head of the department, the Minister, is. Local authorities contain elected members called Councillors. They obviously keep an eye on what the Chief Executive of the Council is up to in their name. Public bodies are not elected but their work is monitored by the Scrutiny Committee and presumably by the regulatory body attached to their industry. The general public is also fairly effective in bringing bad law to the attention of their elected representatives or at least to that of the local newspaper. Make sure you mention all these points and then put forward a well thought through and balanced opinion of your own.

Unit 5

Statutory interpretation

Why do I need to know about statutory interpretation?

Questions will ask you about the key elements of statutory interpretation but also will require an evaluation of the system and how far judges are bound by previous legal decisions. You will need to use cases to support your arguments. Statutory interpretation involves the use of rules and different approaches. Do not take these as being too strict. Judges have flexibility in the way they interpret. There are also some

Which one are they talking about?

Latin phrases associated with interpretation. Learn the spellings and put the phrases onto index cards. The concepts are the most important thing to understand; you will need to be able to apply them in the case study material you will be presented with in the examination.

1 | Statutory interpretation

Statutory interpretation and judges

Drafting legal documents is a time-consuming and difficult task. Sometimes the more you look at a piece of writing that you have done, the less you see. With legal documents, accuracy and clear meaning are of great importance. As with most things in life, however, tiny mistakes creep in or things happen that the drafter could never have imagined. It is left to judges to interpret the law. In other words, judges must use their experience and skill to make the best use they can of the law to ensure a fair and just outcome to a case. The process of working out the meanings of the words in Acts of Parliament or in other legislation is known as *statutory interpretation*. Parliament passes laws, and judges interpret them and put them into operation.

Some help is given to judges within the legislation itself. Some help comes from following certain rules. Finally the passing of the **Interpretation Act 1978** has provided judges with some guidance to help them in this difficult task.

Problems of interpretation

There are a variety of reasons why judges need to interpret the law to bring out its full meaning.

The *subtleties of language* encourage disputes about the meanings of words. English is particularly disposed to this, and legal language is even trickier. Ordinary words that are spelt exactly the same often have different meanings. For example, the word *jumper* can mean someone hopping up and down or an item of clothing. There are thousands of words that have a double meaning, and no matter how hard the writers of law try, they cannot avoid including some. The position is not helped when lawyers deliberately attempt to seek out and exploit these confusions to support their client.

The *passage of time* can make some words redundant or change words from their original meaning. Some laws remain on the books for decades or longer, so the scope for this is great. This is probably one reason why legal terminology sounds so old-fashioned and out of date to some.

In normal communication you can ask the other person to clarify what they mean, but this is impossible with the law. The law makers cannot be questioned about what they meant after the law has been passed. Judges have to do their best to uncover the meaning or investigate if it is unclear.

New inventions and new situations mean that legislation is sometimes used in unfamiliar situations, so judges have to use the law flexibly. This is often the case with technological or social changes. The use of e-mails, the Internet and certain recreational drugs has forced judges to make do with existing laws until new ones can be produced.

Our own *racial, religious, social, political and family perspectives* make us see words, ideas and laws in different ways. This requires the judges to do their best to find some common ground on the meaning of the law.

Jargon buster

A *statute* is another name for an Act of Parliament. **Statutory interpretation** therefore relates to interpreting these statutes or Acts of Parliament.

Examination tip

Work with other students to build up your commitment. Encourage each other as a team. Difficult concepts are more easily understood with a number of people working on them.

Changes in technology cannot be foreseen

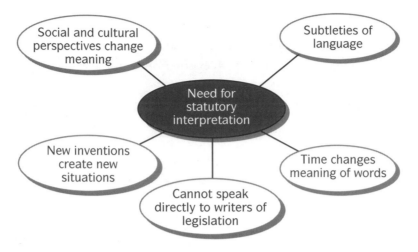

The need for statutory interpretation

2 Rules used when interpreting

There are three broad approaches to the interpretation of legislation. A judge may choose which one to adopt or may even use all three at different stages in the interpretation.

The literal rule

The *literal rule* involves looking at the dictionary definition of the words and using these ordinary meanings, even if the result is illogical or silly. There are some advantages to this method, however.

- **Certainty** – We can all probably agree on the ordinary meaning of words, and the 'meaning' of the law is not interpreted or interfered with by the judge. He or she obeys the strict letter of the law.

- **Reduction of litigation** – Laws are often tested in the court to clarify or even change their meanings. The literal approach makes this testing unnecessary.

- **Constitutional position** – If the judges obey the letter of the law, no one can say they are defying the right of Parliament to have its will done. Parliament is the supreme law maker and the literal approach helps it maintain this view.

There are also some disadvantages of using the literal rule.

- **Uncertainty of words** – The rule does not take into account the nature of language. The words we use have ambiguities attached to them that we experience every day.

- **Problems of drafting law** – People are not perfect, including those who draft and make our laws. Mistakes will be made, no matter how hard people try. The job of the person drafting legislation is to minimize the errors as much as possible, but there will always be mistakes.

The literal rule

- **Lack of flexibility** – Flexibility is the key to all effective and long-lasting systems. The literal approach avoids this suppleness and may make the system unfair and open to exploitation or damage.

The golden rule

If the legislation throws up two possible meanings or an absurdity, the *golden rule* says to choose the one which is least bizarre or look for the sensible meaning. The golden rule was defined by Lord Blackburn in 1877 when he said that the court should take the literal meaning unless it led to an absurdity. In this case the court should use its common sense and choose the most sensible interpretation.

There is a problem, however, with the golden rule if the judge thinks there is an absurdity because he or she does not like the law. The judge may then see absurdities where perhaps none exist.

Legal case: R v Allen (1872)

Allen was accused of bigamy, which means marrying a person while you are still married to another. The law seemed to suggest that he could not marry as he was already married. This would mean that no one could ever commit the offence of bigamy once they had married. The law was interpreted to mean 'going through with a marriage ceremony'. Allen was found guilty.

The mischief rule

The *mischief rule* attempts to understand what Parliament meant. It tries to find out what wrong or mischief the law was trying to correct. For example, the **Theft Act 1968** was intended to prevent people from stealing and to ensure that ordinary citizens do not lose their property. If a misleading paragraph in the legislation went against this and rewarded the thief and punished the innocent victim, then the court would know there was something wrong if it used the mischief rule.

A key case in developing the mischief rule was *Heydon's Case (1584)*. The case encouraged judges to:

● look at the previous law

● explore what was wrong with that law

● identify how Parliament intended to bring about improvements

● apply the findings to the case they were considering.

Smith v Hughes (1960) shows how this was used more recently.

Legal case: Smith v Hughes (1960)

In 1958, the law made it illegal for prostitutes to use the street to find customers for their services (soliciting); it specifically mentioned 'streets'. A defence was put up that the prostitute was hanging out of her window overlooking the street and was therefore innocent of breaking the law. The court used the mischief rule and declared that it was the will of Parliament to avoid the nuisance caused by the actions of the prostitutes whether in the street or hanging out of the window.

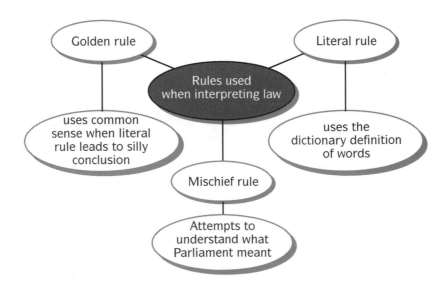

Rules used when interpreting law

Purposive approach

The latest development of these three ways of interpreting is called the *purposive approach* (looking for the purpose). It is very much along the lines of the mischief approach in that it looks for what Parliament intended. The court looks for what it thinks Parliament intended and applies it to the case in hand. The starting point for the process of interpretation is of course still the words themselves.

Legal case: Royal College of Nursing v Department of Health and Social Security (1981)

The **Abortion Act 1967** made abortion legal for the first time in the UK. There were a number of conditions attached when the law was passed. One of these was that a 'registered medical practitioner' must perform the operation. This was taken to mean a doctor. Over the years drugs were developed which meant that nurses were more than capable of performing and monitoring the procedure. The law lords came to the conclusion that the intention of Parliament was to avoid illegal abortions ('back street' abortions). This meant that nurses could now perform the procedure since they worked in a legitimate medical environment.

Did you know?

The name of a legal case is written like this: *Smith v Hughes (1960)*. The first name shows who is bringing the case, *v* means *versus* (against), and the second name shows who the case is brought against. In cases such as *R v Allen (1872)*, *R* stands for *Regina* (Queen) and means the Government.

Revision card activity

Using index cards, make notes on the pros and cons of the literal approach.

Examination tip

Although these aids to interpretation are called *rules*, the judges use them only if they are helpful. They are not compulsory.

Group activity

The 'morning after' pill can be bought over the counter at chemists' shops or obtained free on prescription from doctors' surgeries. Do you think this development means the issue of abortion methods and presence of a registered medical practitioner needs clarification in court?

Clearly, the interpretation of law has always been an issue. Some rules and guidance have come about to help when dealing with language.

- The *ejusdem generis* principle means that a word takes its meaning from the words around it. A list of words referring to cars, such as hatchback, sports, saloon, convertible, and family, will not then include a two-wheeled motorbike. The word takes its meaning from the specific words mentioned as examples.

- The *expressio unius exclusio alterius* principle means that the inclusion of one type of item excludes others. The **Channel Tunnel Act** (1986) refers only to that one tunnel and not to others that may be constructed.

- The *noscitur a sociis* principle means that the word should be interpreted within the context. The paragraph, section or Act itself will give guidance as to the words' meaning.

Revision card activity

Using index cards, note the three rules of interpretation used by judges. Even if you have difficulty remembering the phrases, try to remember the concepts.

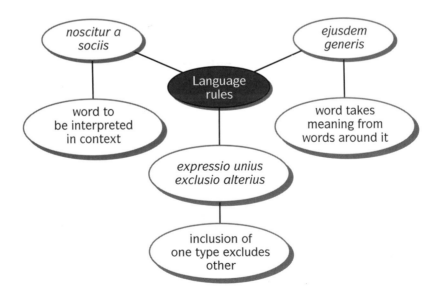

Language rules

4 | Presumptions when interpreting law

There are three key presumptions (*assumptions*) that the judge will take for granted when interpreting the law.

- *Mens rea* (the mental element) is required for a crime to be committed.

- The common law has not changed.

- There is no retrospective law (someone cannot be charged with an offence that did not exist when they carried it out).

These presumptions will hold unless it can be argued that they should not.

Examination tip

Make sure you share your time in the exam according to the number of marks available for each question.

5 | Intrinsic and extrinsic aids

Judges can also call upon further support when interpreting. The nature of this support is slowly changing, partly due to our membership of the EU and the European legal system. The European Court of Justice interprets law slightly differently, relying upon a wider range of external aids. This is gradually having an influence in the UK.

Intrinsic aids

These are aids which are *internal* to the legislation. They are present inside the Act of Parliament itself to help with the interpretation of the law.

- The name of the Act gives the objectives of the piece of legislation and at times can be long and detailed to avoid misinterpretation of these objectives.

- Sometimes there are detailed definitions of the words used in the Act to ensure everyone is focused on the right meaning.

- Marginal notes are used to guide the reader in the right direction.

- Interpretation sections give guidance on areas where there may be problems.

Extrinsic aids

These are aids which are *external* to the legislation.

- The *Oxford English Dictionary* is particularly useful if judges are making use of the literal rule. It can, of course, help in all situations to have a definition of legal terms from such a reputable source.

- Official Government documentation is used, such as Green Papers (first draft ideas) and White Papers (later firmer proposals for discussion).

- Law Commission Reports give information on the reasons for possible changes in the law, and judges may use these sources to better inform themselves of the origin of the concern that led to a change in the law.

- Other statutes which relate to or went before the one they are exploring give the judges a context to use when considering a case.

- *Hansard* is the official record of parliamentary debates. All speeches and statements are recorded in *Hansard*. It may be useful for judges to read the debates by members of the House of Commons or House of Lords that went before the passing of the Act. They may give some context and insight into the reasons for the law.

- The publications of pressure groups cannot be used to inform the debate. Only official publications are allowed.

Legal case: Pepper v Hart (1993)

Confusion over the meaning of the **Finance Act 1976** meant that teachers who were possibly entitled to a tax allowance seemed to be losing out. The court eventually went to the record of the debate in Parliament which made it clear what the intention of the legislation was. This was a breakthrough in the use of *Hansard* for court use. The teachers got their tax allowance.

Web activity

Look for *Hansard* on the Internet. Explore the details of a debate to see the format that is used in parliamentary debates.

6 The European Union and the literal and purposive debate

There have been movements over time in what is the most fashionable method of interpreting legislation. The present trend is towards a more purposive approach. This has partly come about because of a more flexible attitude towards interpretation, giving the mischief rule more priority over the literal rule, and also because of the influence of the European Union.

The European Court of Justice has a purposive attitude towards the interpretation of law. The interpretation of European law is supported by frequent reference to official European Parliamentary and institutional sources. This has had its effect on the operations of the English judiciary. They are under an obligation to interpret European law with the purposive approach, and now tend to use this approach with English law too. In addition, English courts can make use of a variety of extrinsic (external) aids, including international conventions and *travaux preparatories* (preparatory legal materials). All of these developments have moved the interpretation of law clearly away from literal interpretations and towards the purposive camp.

Revision checklist

1 The interpretation of law is required because: language can be ambiguous, we are not able to clarify law with the makers, new situations arise, words are bound up with cultural values.

2 Judges attempt to interpret the meaning of the law and are helped by the **Interpretation Act 1978**.

3 Three approaches to interpretation are the literal, golden and mischief rules.

4 Approach most in favour now is called purposive, which is very similar to the mischief rule.

5 Rules of language: *ejusdem generis* (word takes meaning from those around it), *expressio unius exclusio alterius* (inclusion of one type excludes others) and *noscitur a sociis* (word must be interpreted within context).

6 Presumptions when interpreting law: *mens rea* required, common law has not changed and no retrospective law.

7 Intrinsic (internal) aids include: name of the act, definitions of words, notes in the margins and interpretation sections.

8 Extrinsic (external) aids include: dictionaries, official relevant Government publications, Law Commission Reports, other statutes and *Hansard*.

9 European Union membership has encouraged purposive approach to interpretation because European Court of Justice takes this approach.

10 English courts use a variety of extrinsic aids, including international conventions and preparatory materials.

Quick revision questions

1   What are the main causes of disputes about the meaning of legislation?

2   Name some advantages to the literal rule.

3   What is the golden rule?

4   What did *Heydon's Case (1584)* illustrate?

5   What is the purposive approach?

6   What do these terms mean: *ejusdem generis*; *expressio unius exclusio alterius*; *noscitur a sociis*?

7   What are the three main presumptions judges make when interpreting?

8   Name some intrinsic aids.

9   Name some extrinsic aids.

10   What approach does the European Court of Justice take to interpretation of legislation?

Exam questions

1   *a*   Outline the meaning of the term *literal rule*. (10 marks)

    b   Comment on the problems that might arise in using the literal rule. (20 marks)

Exam answer guide

1 *a* The literal rule relies on using the dictionary definition of words contained in legislation. It looks only at the meaning of the words used and not at their context or the purpose of the legislators. There are some advantages of the literal approach including:

✓ Certainty of meaning with the use of commonly used words

✓ Reduction of litigation since there are no legal terms to clarify in court

✓ Constitutional position means the courts are not going against the will of Parliament.

This is an approach which is losing favour, partly due to a more flexible approach from judges in the interpretation of the law but also because the European Court of Justice favours the purposive approach.

b Significant problems may arise in using the literal approach:

✓ Uncertainty of words means that the literal approach may bring about an unjust interpretation of the law.

✓ Problems of drafting law mean mistakes will always be present. Possibly judges should attempt to iron these out.

✓ Lack of flexibility means that judges do not use common sense, even when the meaning may be clear to all.

Part b contains the bulk of marks for this question, so concentrate your resources here and comment on the literal approach.

Unit 6

The doctrine of judicial precedent

Why do I need to know about judicial precedent?

Questions on judicial precedent will require you to be familiar with the court hierarchy and how it operates. The **1966 Practice Statement**, which affects how the House of Lords operates, and the jurisdiction of the European Court of Justice are also essential issues. It is crucial that you know the differences between important terms such as *stare decisis*, *ratio decidendi* and *obiter dicta* and how they will affect the judge's eventual decision. Judicial precedent is a critical area to understand and illustrates the predictability and flexibility of the English legal system.

Judicial precedent

Precedent as operated in the English Courts

Most cases that come before a court are similar to cases heard before. There are probably only so many crimes and ways that they can be committed. If the facts of a case are similar enough, then prosecutors, defenders and judges can use the legal arguments and decisions from these earlier cases. There are some clear advantages arising from this approach.

- **Fairness** – Each case is treated the same if the facts are close enough to each other. This means that there are no wild variations between similar cases. A person who commits a crime today will be treated the same as someone who commits a similar crime next year.

- **Consistency** – There is consistency between cases that strengthens the system and also allows for some prediction of the result. Those contemplating crime will know that there will be certain consequences if they are caught.

- **Saving time** – The system saves time for all those involved in the case. The arguments have already been analysed and decided upon.

- **Source of law** – Precedent produces a valuable source of law within which legal personnel can operate. It provides a foundation for the legal system and is particularly useful for the training of lawyers. Case law provides approximately 400 000 examples of individuals and their stories within the legal system.

- **Real life** – Case law is real life. Law that comes from this source is not subject to problems of drafting, which often occur with parliamentary legislation.

There are also disadvantages arising from this approach.

- **Vast choice of cases** – The use of the Internet has improved the situation, but the judge is still faced with a vast number of cases to choose from. Some cases are not, of course, yet on the system. These latter cases can only be used with the permission of the court they were heard in.

- **Inflexibility** – Instead of looking at each case afresh, previous decisions have to be used. This might reduce the freshness with which each case is looked at. It also reduces the chance of law developing as society develops. What was criminal behaviour in Victorian times might not be seen in the same light in 2003.

- **Disputes** – There may be disputes about whether the previous case applies to the new situation. Defence lawyers and prosecution lawyers may have very different views on which case is appropriate to use as an authority. The judge is left to choose between them.

Donoghue v Stevenson (1932) and *Daniels v White (1938)* illustrate precedent.

Legal case: Donoghue v Stevenson (1932)

Two friends visited a café and one drank a bottle of ginger beer. When the remains of the bottle of beer were poured into the glass, out came a decomposed snail. The woman felt ill and sued the manufacturer for this unpleasant experience. She won the case.

Legal case: Daniels v White (1938)

The claimant bought a bottle of lemonade and when he drank it, he felt a burning reaction in his throat. The lemonade was examined and was found to contain a corrosive chemical. The case of *Donoghue v Stevenson* was used to sue for compensation for the claimant even though the case was slightly different. It was near enough, however, to use for the purposes of precedent.

Quick question

List the strengths and weaknesses of using the principle of judicial precedent.

Examination tip

Questions at AS level will often ask you to comment on legal principles. This means looking at the pros and cons and giving your opinion.

Donoghue and Stevenson (1932)

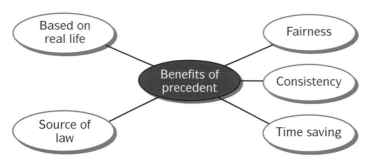

The benefits of precedent

Judicial precedent in practice

The legal system is full of rules and regulations which give the system its strength and predictability. The process of making decisions on judicial precedent is helped by certain rules that are kept. There are three key conventions.

Stare decisis

Stare decisis means 'let the previous decision stand'. Points of law that have been decided in previous similar cases must be followed. This makes the system consistent, fair and predictable. Another part to *stare decisis* is that higher courts take priority over lower courts, that is, higher courts **bind** lower courts. Stare decisis:

- allows previous decisions to influence later similar cases
- ensures that higher courts bind lower courts.

Obiter dicta

When a judge makes a judgment on a case, they may give many supporting arguments and explanations as to why they will come to a particular decision. This introductory stage, or anything else that is said by the judge, which is not a central part to the judgment but is put in to make the situation clearer, is known as the *obiter dicta*. The *obiter dicta* includes:

- the judge's thought processes
- the judge's explanation as to why one decision was arrived at rather than another
- how the judge is going to apply the decision to the present case.

Ratio decidendi

The *obiter dicta* is the lead-up to the decision and the *ratio decidendi* is the core of the decision itself. This is the part of the decision made by the judge which has the effect of binding later courts. It is the piece later judges need to follow when looking at the case they are trying. The *ratio decidendi*:

- is the core to the decision
- is binding on similar cases heard by later judges.

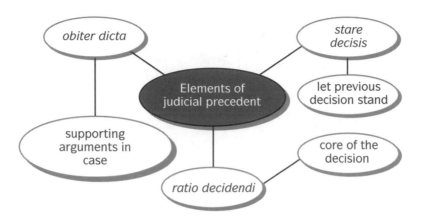

Elements of judicial precedent

Jargon buster

Bind means that there is no choice but to obey. The court is under an obligation to follow the lead set.

Quick question

What do the phrases *stare decisis*, *obiter dicta* and *ratio decidendi* mean? Put your answers onto index cards and memorize them.

Group activity

Get a copy of *The Times* newspaper and find some law reports. Identify the *ratio decidendi* of some cases and note the court making the decision.

Examination tip

Examiners are happy to see you can quote Latin phrases in your work, but they are even happier to see them applied correctly to relevant case studies.

3 | Hierarchy of the courts

One of the fundamental rules of the concept of *stare decisis* is that higher courts take priority over lower courts. The court system has a hierarchy. It has a structure of power from the bottom to the top. Clearly, higher courts such as the House of Lords can tell lower courts what to do. The higher court has more senior and powerful judges sitting in it who can give orders and exert more influence. The civil court system is organized with the most powerful court, the European Court of Justice, at the top (if a point of

European Law is involved) and the most junior court, the County Court, at the bottom.

In the civil system cases begin either in the County Court or the High Court, depending on the amount of money involved, the complexity of the case and the parties involved. The actual case is normally about who did what to whom, or how much A owes B. The case does not normally contest the validity of the law – it just looks at the facts of the argument.

If, when the decision comes, the losing party does not like the result or disputes the fairness of the law, it can go to appeal. This begins what can be a lengthy and very expensive process. Normally only the rich or those backed by an organization such as a union or professional body go down this road.

Appeals are where precedent is most likely to be set. An appeal from the County Court or High Court can go to the Court of Appeal (Civil Division) or eventually to the Judicial Committee of the House of Lords. Whether a case becomes a precedent depends then on two things:

- the existence of a dispute over a point of law between two contesting legal parties

- the ability and the desire of both parties to pursue the matter further. If this is not the case, the legal point is not clarified and lives to be heard another day.

Inferior courts are those below High Court level. They cannot establish precedent. They follow the rulings of the courts above them. The Court of Appeal (Civil Division) and the Court of Appeal (Criminal Division) are bound by their previous rulings to a certain extent. A ruling in *Young v Bristol Aeroplane Company (1944)* led to a certain degree of flexibility.

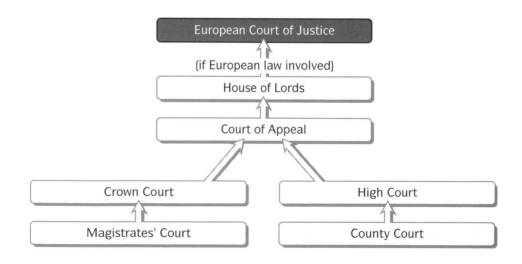

The hierarchy of the courts

The House of Lords is the highest court that sits in the UK. It sets precedent for all courts below it when dealing with English law. It does not always have to follow its own previous decisions since the **Practice Statement of 1966**, which allowed it some flexibility in this area.

The European Court of Justice

The European Court of Justice (ECJ) confines itself to law that involves a European element. A case that starts in the County Court does not have to go through the full range of UK courts before it gets to Luxembourg, which is where the ECJ sits. It can go directly to the ECJ if the case involves a point of European Union law. When a decision is made by the ECJ it is immediately binding on all UK courts.

The ECJ is only involved when there is a point concerning European legislation. If the case involves only English law, then the House of Lords is the highest court where law can be clarified.

Research activity

Using the law sections of newspapers, identify the types of cases heard by the ECJ.

Examination tip

Spell hierarchy properly. Hundreds of students get it wrong each year.

4   Binding and persuasive precedent

The hierarchy of the courts is important in deciding whether the court has to follow the decision of an earlier case. This is known as *binding precedent*. The court's hands are tied! If the earlier case is not binding but may be of interest nevertheless, then it may provide *persuasive precedent*.

Binding precedent

A judgment made on a case will contain various elements: the facts of the case, a statement detailing the legal issues relating to the case (*ratio decidendi*), the legal discussion surrounding the case (*obiter dicta*) and the verdict reached by the judge.

The most important element is the *ratio decidendi*. It is this which effectively binds the judges in later cases. The facts of the case can be used to see the relevance of the case, the *obiter dicta* can be used to understand the issues involved and the verdict may be of interest at the end of the hearing, but it is the *ratio decidendi* alone that binds the court.

Persuasive precedent

A persuasive precedent is a case that may be helpful to a court but which it does not have to follow. The court may be persuaded to follow its legal rulings but is not under any obligation to do so. Persuasive precedent may be:

- the surrounding legal discussion from an earlier case (*obiter dicta*)

- a decision that comes from a lower court in the hierarchy

- decisions from foreign courts, especially Canada, New Zealand and Australia

- a judgment that was made in the Court of Appeal or the House of Lords but which was outvoted by other judges on the panel – such *dissenting views* (those which go against the majority) are published in the English legal system but not in the European Court of Justice.

5 Reporting cases

If judicial precedent is to be effective, judges need information on previous relevant cases. The earliest records of cases date back to the thirteenth century. They were not particularly accurate! Sources available today include:

- The Council of Law Reporting, which was created in 1865 to improve the process of law reporting, still produces the series *Law Reports*.

- Reports of cases published by private companies; the most widely known are the *All England Law Reports*.

- Electronic law reporting is now gaining popularity because of its incredible speed and accuracy; LEXIS is one system.

- The Internet: many websites on the Internet have past legal cases on them.

6 Avoidance of judicial precedent

The legal system reflects the society it regulates. As a result laws must develop and change if they are to be seen as fair and relevant. Offences such as rape within marriage, the legal status of those with different sexual preferences and the official attitude towards drug-taking are areas where the law has developed to reflect more modern thinking. The practice of judicial precedent has important flexibilities built into it to allow room for manoeuvre.

Overruling

Overruling means that a higher court creates a different legal ruling to one made by a previous lower court. The later case is looked at in a different way and the precedent set in the earlier case is set aside. The higher court destroys the earlier precedent when it does this and effectively declares the earlier ruling wrong. The House of Lords can also set aside its own earlier precedent. This was made possible by a device known as the **Practice Statement 1966**. This means that the House of Lords is not bound by its own earlier decisions. Overruling involves:

- Two cases
- Earlier decision on first case discredited by second case
- Higher court involved in decision to change precedent.

Reversing

If an appeal court disputes a decision made in a lower court on a particular case, it is known as *reversing*. A reversal is basically a decision which goes against the decision of the original court. Reversing involves:

- One case
- Goes to appeal
- Court throws out earlier decision.

Distinguishing

If a judge wants to avoid binding precedent set by an earlier case, he or she can try to argue that the facts in the two cases are different. If this is successful, the earlier precedent should not apply to the later case. The judge tries to *distinguish* between the two. Distinguishing involves:

- Two cases
- Judge does not want to follow precedent set in earlier one
- Judge claims the two cases are too different from each other to allow one case to set precedent in the other case.

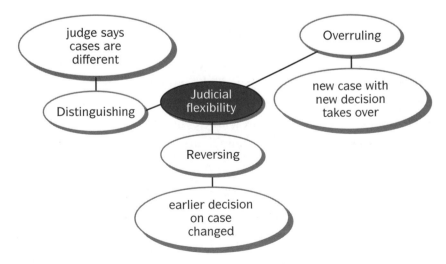

Judicial flexibility

It is important to know how far judges are bound by precedent and how much freedom they have.

Revision checklist

1 Precedent involves using the details and rulings of similar legal cases which have been heard before.

2 Advantages of using precedent are: fairness, consistency, saving time, produces a source of law, and involves real cases.

3 Disadvantages of using precedent are: too many cases to choose from, can lead to inflexibility and staleness, and disputes arise over use of specific cases.

4 *Stare decisis* (let the previous decision stand), *obiter dicta* (words which support the core judgment) and *ratio decidendi* (the core judgement, the essence of the case).

5 The courts have a hierarchy which affects whether precedent is set. Higher courts bind lower courts.

6 Precedent is set when a case involves a dispute over the law and when the parties involved want to take the case higher.

7 The **Practice Statement 1966** allows the House of Lords flexibility not to follow its own previous rulings.

8 Precedent set by the European Court of Justice binds all English courts.

9 Courts have to follow binding precedent but can choose whether or not to follow persuasive precedent.

10 Overruling involves a higher court setting aside a previous precedent, reversing involves going against the findings of an earlier court on that case, and distinguishing involves a judge trying to prove the present case is substantially different from the case which is trying to bind the judge with a precedent.

Quick revision questions

1 Name the key advantages in using judicial precedent.

2 Why would a defence lawyer argue about which case should be used for precedent?

3 How can *obiter dicta* be used?

4 What are the advantages to using *stare decisis*?

5 What is the *ratio decidendi* of a case?

6 Draw the civil court structure.

7 What role does the ECJ play in the English legal system?

8 What is the difference between binding and persuasive precedent?

9 What are the differences between overruling, reversing and distinguishing?

10 In which newspaper can you find law reports?

Exam question

1 *a* Outline the process of judicial precedent. (15 marks)

  b Why might precedent cause problems for the development of the law? (15 marks)

Exam answer guide

1 *a* The process of precedent relies on judges finding cases which have similar facts and then applying the earlier ruling to the later case. The judge may find information on previous cases from:

✓ The Internet

✓ CD ROMs

✓ LEXIS

✓ *All England Law Reports*

✓ Law reports

✓ Newspapers.

Lawyers will probably argue with the judge on which cases to use for precedent, but it is the judge who has the final say.

b The following arguments can be made.

✓ Precedent can be binding or persuasive. If it is binding it may limit the judge's ability to give new and fresh judgments. The House of Lords was once bound by its past decisions, which some thought limited the scope for law development.

✓ On the other hand, judges can get around this by distinguishing the case, i.e. saying it is different from the one being tried. The higher courts can overrule and reverse decisions. The House of Lords can use the 1966 Practice Statement to get out of its earlier decisions.

Give both sides and then state your own opinion. Overall, is the use of precedent a beneficial state of affairs or not?

Unit 7 European legislative processes and institutions

Why do I need to know about European legislation and European institutions?

Questions on European law will test your understanding of the various European Union legal and political institutions and will also probe your understanding of parliamentary sovereignty and legal supremacy. In other words, is English law or European law more important? Which one takes priority if there is a clash? In fact, a great deal of European law automatically becomes effective in the United Kingdom as

Europe

soon as it is passed in Europe. Other pieces of European legislation have to be put into place by the United Kingdom. Whatever route is taken, all businesses, employers, consumers and governments are eventually affected by European law. You are expected to put a balanced, fair and intelligent view on the importance and drawbacks of European law.

1 The birth and development of the European Union

The European Union is a group of powerful, western European countries who have been drawn closer to each other by a set of agreements. These agreements cover economic, business, trade and even military issues. The countries believe that they are more powerful and more prosperous when they act as a group rather than as individual countries. The cement that holds these agreements together is European Union law.

Reasons for the birth of the European Union

During the twentieth century unimaginable loss of life, injury and physical destruction came to Europe twice, during two world wars. The first lasted from 1914 to 1918 and the second from 1939 to 1945. Both of these terrible wars started in Europe but in the end spread to much of the world, including the United States and the Soviet Union (now known as Russia). After the Second World War, European leaders tried to find a way of cooperating on economic, social and even political issues. A European legal system was to play two important roles in the future safety and prosperity of Europe.

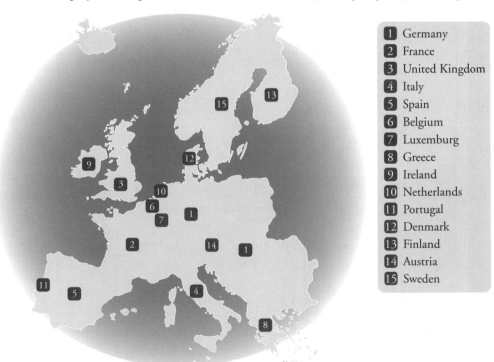

1 Germany
2 France
3 United Kingdom
4 Italy
5 Spain
6 Belgium
7 Luxemburg
8 Greece
9 Ireland
10 Netherlands
11 Portugal
12 Denmark
13 Finland
14 Austria
15 Sweden

The countries of the EU in 2002

1 It would provide a *legal framework* for the objectives and agreements of the European Union. Politicians would discuss such issues as improving workers rights, extending consumer protection and safeguarding the environment. Each of these key areas needed European legislation to guide and enforce the proposals.

2 European law would provide a *legal rather than military solution* to problems that would inevitably crop up between neighbouring countries. During a dispute countries could put forward their legal case to the European Court of Justice. The judges would look at the strengths of both cases and give a legal decision or attempt some sort of solution to the problem. This would be far more satisfactory than a military invasion.

Over the past 50 years European law has become an important source of law in the United Kingdom and in the rest of the European Union. European law and its legal institutions have played a vital part in the development of the European Union, allowing member states to solve disputes in the court rather than on the battlefield. For the first time in many centuries peace amongst the major European powers has been possible, in part because of the cooperation encouraged by the European Union and its developing legal system.

2 The major institutions of the European Union

The European parliamentary system is very different from our own. Institutions that we are familiar with in the UK have very different functions in Europe. It is important to read the description of each carefully.

The Council of Ministers

The main decision-making and law-making body of the European Union is the Council of Ministers. This is therefore the most powerful part of the European Union structure.

The number of votes each country can use is based on its total population. This is called *weighting*. To ensure fairness the five big countries (the 'Big Five' are Germany, France, the UK, Spain and Italy) always have to get the support of smaller countries to win a vote. This ensures that smaller members have their say and that big countries do not always win issues beneficial to them.

The member states normally send their Foreign Ministers as their representatives to the Council of Ministers. The Foreign Minister will speak for the interests of his or her country within the Council of Ministers.

Since the Foreign Minister has many other responsibilities back home, there is a committee of diplomats who act as representatives when the Foreign Ministers are not there. They do the day-to-day work so that when Ministers do meet they discuss only the most important and urgent matters. The committee is known as the Committee of Permanent Representatives.

Some meetings of the Council of Ministers discuss specific issues. A minister may deal better with these meetings if they come from a particular department. If, for example, the Council is discussing the beef ban caused by BSE or the spread of foot and mouth disease in Europe, then the Agriculture Minister from each member state would attend the meeting instead. Finally, if the Prime Ministers of the member countries meet, the meeting is called a *summit*.

The European Commission

The European Commission acts on behalf of the interests of the European Union. The Commission's key job is to propose legislation. Although each commissioner comes from a member country, he or she puts aside the interest of their own country and focuses on the interests of all fifteen European member states. The Commission consists of twenty commissioners. The 'Big Five' countries have two commissioners each, while smaller countries such as Luxembourg have one commissioner each. Each commissioner holds their post for five years and has responsibility for a particular area. One of our commissioners, Neil Kinnock, is at present Vice-President of the Commission.

The European Parliament

The European Parliament is very different from our own House of Commons and House of Lords. It is a place for discussing and commenting on the legislation that is passing through the European legislative system. This process is known as *consultation*. Consultation does not mean that feedback has to be incorporated into final decisions.

The European Parliament does, however, have some important powers.

● It has the power to investigate the Council of Ministers and the Commission.

● It can dismiss the Commission and has the right to refuse the commissioners put forward by member countries.

In 1999 the European Parliament dismissed the whole Commission because there had been serious allegations of fraud and other misbehaviour. Many members who were dismissed are, however, back in their original jobs.

The European Court of Justice

The European Union is one of the most powerful organizations in the world and has its own legal system. It therefore has its own court – the European Court of Justice. This European Union court is often confused with another important court in Europe, the European Court of Human Rights, but this is an entirely separate court.

The European Court of Justice (ECJ) has two main aims:

● to ensure that European law is interpreted efficiently

● to ensure that European law is applied fairly and effectively.

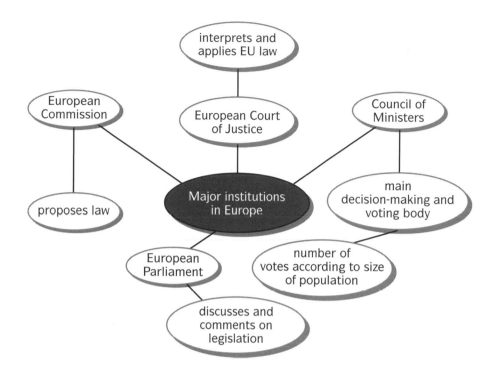

Major institutions in Europe

The European Court of Justice consists of fifteen judges, one from each EU member state. Nine other legal experts, called Advocates General, advise the judges.

European Court of Justice

- If everyone supports a piece of legislation the vote is said to be *unanimous*. This can sometimes be difficult to achieve since there are at the moment fifteen members of the European Union. The Council will sometimes accept a majority of votes to pass a piece of legislation.

- If one country disagrees then some types of legislation cannot be passed. If a country votes against a law in this way, it is called a *veto*.

3 Sources and terminology of EU law

Primary sources: Treaties of the European Union and regulations

These are the main source of European Law. Essentially they are important agreements made by the member states. *Treaties* give power to the various institutions within the European Union, set the direction for the European Union to follow and define the rights and responsibilities of member states. Examples of treaties include:

- The Treaty of Rome (1957), which essentially formed the European Union and gave it its legal status

- The Maastricht Treaty (1992)

- The Treaty of Amsterdam (1997)

- The Treaty of Nice (2001), which explored the possibilities and issues surrounding enlargement of the European Union.

Regulations are rules which must be obeyed automatically by all member states. They make sure that there is consistency throughout the European Union since every country has to obey the same law. Regulation 1251/70, for example allows workers and their families the right to live in any EU country.

Secondary sources: directives, decisions and case law

- A *directive* lays down a goal. It is up to each member state to decide how the goal is best achieved. The UK Government normally uses something called delegated legislation to meet the requirements of European directives.

- *Decisions* normally relate to a particular country or individual.

- *Case law* is generated by the European Court of Justice. Unlike in the English legal system, decisions do not become binding on later cases the ECJ hears.

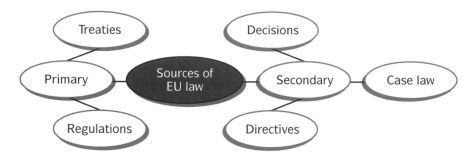

Sources of law

4 Areas covered by EU law

In the short time that European law has existed, it has made important strides into areas that affect individual European citizens, businesses and governments. Legislation has been passed which covers:

- **The free movement of workers within the EU** – No worker should be prevented from taking up a job anywhere in the EU if he or she has the qualifications and experience and is wanted by the employer.

- **The free movement of goods and services within the EU** – No business should have a tax or tariff on its goods that makes it more difficult for it to trade than a company within another member state.

- **Issues of sexual equality in the work place** – Equal pay and the status of part-time (mostly women) workers have been a particular focus.

- **Health and Safety matters within EU businesses and organizations** – The EU is keen to protect the health and safety interests of EU workers.

- **Competition policy within member states** – This prevents unfair competition from large companies that want to dominate certain markets. Competition policy even affects governments who want to bail out struggling companies. (This caused serious problems for airlines after the World Trade Centre bombings.)

- **Law and order** – These initiatives often apply to the movements of football hooligans and faster deportation of criminals from one EU member state to another.

- **Military and anti-terrorist issues** – There is no European army, but closer cooperation has been developing and there are already many structures for sharing anti-terrorist information.

- **Trade issues** – The EU is one of the few blocks of countries that can stand up to the enormous commercial and political strength of the United States. The US talks directly to EU officials rather than to individual member states.

- **Environmental issues** – Environmental damage is no respecter of boundaries, so it is far more effective to develop Europe-wide solutions to these problems.

Trade is a legal and political issue

Areas covered by EU legislation

5 Implementation of EU law

The English courts must enforce all of these laws and provisions. Furthermore, domestic English courts now have a duty to implement EU law in any case where it differs to English law. There are a number of ways that European law, proposed by the Commission, discussed by the Parliament and voted on by the Council, actually becomes law in the UK.

Directly applicable

A legal action or defence involving a provision of European law can be brought in a national court if it is directly applicable. This means that the provision is automatically part of the national law of each member state. Individual member states do not have to go through a legislative process to make a directly applicable piece of legislation enforceable.

Direct effect

A piece of legislation is directly effective if it creates individual rights which can be enforced in the national courts. There are two types of direct effect.

- **Vertical direct effect** creates rights against the state.

- **Horizontal direct effect** creates rights against other individuals.

Quick question

What do the following terms mean: directly applicable, direct effect, vertical direct effect and horizontal direct effect?

6 Effects of EU law on the English legal system

The law of the European Union takes priority over the law of individual member states. *Van Gend en Loos v Netherlands (1962)* paved the way for this position.

Legal case: Van Gend en Loos v Netherlands (1962)

The government of the Netherlands attempted to introduce new customs duties. A ruling by the European Court of Justice prevented this from happening and in doing so established the supremacy of EU law over national law.

The **European Communities Act 1972** (effective from 1 January 1973) states that law created by the European Union becomes UK law. This means that law-making bodies in the EU can make laws that are consequently applicable in the UK. Any disputes about the meaning of these laws are eventually sorted out by the European Court of Justice. If the UK Parliament were to pass a law that went directly against EU law, then the ECJ would find the UK in breach of its duties and take action against it.

Factortame v Secretary of State (1989) is an important case that illustrates the view of the English courts in relation to legislation that came into conflict with Europe.

Legal case: Factortame v Secretary of State (1989)

The European Court of Justice ordered the House of Lords (the highest court in the English legal system) to suspend the operation of the **Merchant Shipping Act 1988** because it had come into conflict with articles of the Treaty of Rome (1957). The House of Lords obeyed the ruling and thereby acknowledged the supremacy of the ECJ over the House of Lords.

It is important to realize that the European Court of Justice is there primarily to assist with the interpretation and application of European law. It is not a final court of appeal on English law. Its consideration is European law alone.

Group activity

What benefits does the UK receive from having a strong European Court of Justice?

Examination tips

● Quoting European case law will give depth to your work and earn extra marks.

● Learn to spell *supremacy* properly.

● The use of past papers is essential for putting your knowledge into practice. Listen carefully to any feedback you receive.

European law

One of the most important areas that European legislation has become involved in is the protection of workers' rights. The working time directive is one specific example of this. Workers are not normally allowed to work more than 48 hours per week. There are some exceptions to this rule and workers can, if they wish, work more than this provided they give their written permission.

Revision checklist

1 The European Union was created to improve economic and political cooperation between powerful western European states and thus avoid the destruction of war.

2 The main institutions of the European Union are the Commission, the European Parliament and the Council of Ministers.

3 The Commission proposes and drafts legislation.

4 The European Parliament discusses the legislation and gives its views. It does not vote on whether it is accepted or not.

5 The Council of Ministers votes on the legislation. Votes are weighted according to the population size of each member state.

6 The main sources of EU legislation are treaties, regulations, directives, decisions and case law.

7 EU law covers a wide range of issues including: free movement of workers, free movement of goods and services, anti-discrimination, health and safety, competition policy, law and order, military and anti-terrorist measures, trade issues and environmental matters.

8 EU law becomes law in the UK through direct effect and directly applicable means.

9 The **European Communities Act 1972** brought the UK into the EU.

10 *Factortame v Secretary of State (1989)* established the supremacy of the European Court of Justice in the UK.

Quick revision questions

1 What is the European Union?

2 What does the Council of Ministers do?

3 What does weighting do?

4 What do the Foreign Ministers do within the Council?

5 Whose interests do the Commissioners look after?

6 What are the key jobs of the Commission?

7 What powers has the European Parliament got?

8 What is the job of the European Court of Justice (ECJ)?

9 How does the ECJ create law?

10 How many judges sit on the ECJ?

Exam questions

1 *a* What are the roles of the following European institutions:

   i   The Council of Ministers

   ii The European Parliament

   iii The European Court of Justice? (15 marks)

   b Is the system of law making in the European Union an effective one in terms of accountability? (15 marks)

Exam answer guide

1 *a* The following can be used as a guide:

   ✓ The Council of Ministers is the key decision-making body of the EU. It votes on legislation which is suggested to it by the European Commission after the European Parliament has been consulted.

   ✓ The European Parliament discusses and comments on the legislation passed to it by the Commission. The Commission and the Council of Ministers are not bound by the views of the Parliament but the views are taken seriously. The Parliament has power to make life difficult for the Commission and can investigate Ministers in the Council.

   ✓ The European Court of Justice interprets and applies European law. It is not bound by its own past decisions. Its findings are binding on all courts in the European Union.

   b Although the European Parliament has no voting powers, the ministers from each member state have. They are democratically elected, so have the backing of the voters at home. The Parliament has the power to investigate (the Ministers) and dismiss (the Commission) so it has some teeth. Checks and balances are in place to stop any of the elements from getting too powerful and abusing their power. Each element is accountable (has to answer) to someone.

Module 2 Dispute Solving

1 Lay people – magistrates and juries

2 The legal profession – barristers, solicitors and legal executives

3 The judges

4 The finance of legal services

5 The criminal courts

6 The civil courts

7 Alternatives to the courts

The legal world

Unit 1
Lay people – magistrates and juries

Why do I need to know about lay people?

Examination questions on lay people will expect you to refer to both magistrates and juries. Lay people underpin the current legal system, and you will need to demonstrate an understanding of how they are selected and appointed. You will need to know what a lay person's duties are and what proposals for reform are currently under review. You should be able to identify strengths and weaknesses in the system and comment on suggested improvements. The Auld Report is essential reading in this area. This unit explores not only the current system but also key proposals affecting lay people.

The jury

1 The selection and training of lay magistrates

The word 'lay' describes a person who is not formally qualified, but is non-professional or amateur. The English legal system relies heavily on such people in the administration of justice. They are felt to bring the system 'down to earth' and allow the 'ordinary person' an opportunity to participate in the machinery of justice.

Lay **magistrates** are part-time judges who hear minor criminal cases at the local Magistrates' Court. Lay magistrates are not legally qualified. They do, however, receive training to help them with their duties. There are about 30 000 lay magistrates in the English legal system and they listen to approximately 98 per cent of all criminal cases and refer the rest to higher courts.

Selection

Anyone between the ages of 21 and 60 may be considered as a candidate to be a magistrate. In reality, however, few people under the age of 27 are called upon for interview. A local Advisory Committee considers applications, interviews candidates and puts forward suitable names to the **Lord Chancellor's Department**. It is hoped that the candidates elected as lay magistrates by the Lord Chancellor will represent a broad range of the local community.

The Lord Chancellor's Department has listed some important qualities that it believes magistrates should have. Magistrates must:

- be of good character

- have personal integrity

- have sound common sense

- have the ability to weigh up evidence and reach a conclusion

- be able to work as a member of a team

- be firm yet compassionate.

Magistrates must live within fifteen miles of the Court and have lived in the locality for a minimum of one year. Magistrates must have a good local knowledge of the area and the people they are dealing with.

There has been some criticism of the lack of balance between different social groups within the magistracy. Magistrates are more often than not middle-class, middle-aged professionals. Some people question whether they can understand the problems of defendants, who often have socially and economically underprivileged backgrounds.

Certain people are not allowed to become magistrates. They include:

- people not of good character and standing

- **undischarged bankrupts**

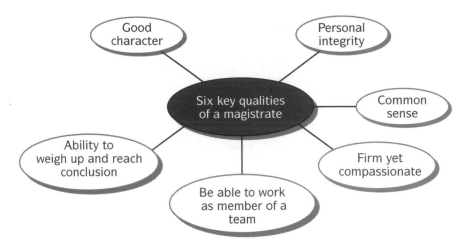

Qualities needed to be a magistrate

- members of the armed forces
- members of the Police
- traffic wardens
- close relatives of someone on the same bench
- anyone who cannot carry out the duties because of a disability.

Training

Training is now a key area of concern for the Lord Chancellor's Department. Inconsistent sentences and verdicts have led to concerns about the support and training given to magistrates. Magistrates are given some training before they listen to and decide on cases. They now continue to receive training throughout their service. A recent scheme, known as the Magistrates' New Training Initiative (MNTI), has developed a mentor-based process. It is hoped that MNTI will provide support for new magistrates by helping them to understand basic law and procedure, develop skills in making fair but firm judgments and develop team-working skills.

Recent events such as the **Human Rights Act 1998** and the publication of the far-reaching Stephen Lawrence Enquiry have focused attention once again on the importance of high-quality training for those working in the magistrates' system.

All the training undertaken by magistrates takes place in their own time, in the evenings and at weekends. The extra training required of magistrates when the **Human Rights Act** came into force led many magistrates to resign.

Revision card activity

Summarize the selection and training of lay magistrates.

Jargon buster

- **Magistrates** are also sometimes also known as Justices of the Peace or JPs. They first appeared in 1361. They were ordered by the King to 'guard the peace'.

- The **Lord Chancellor's Department** is responsible for the running of the court system. The Lord Chancellor, an important legal and political figure, is in charge.

- An **undischarged bankrupt** is a person who is unable to pay their debts and is under the control of a court. The person may choose to declare themselves bankrupt or may be taken to court by a person who is owed money.

Did you know?

- Although lay magistrates have been on the scene for many hundreds of years, the first woman to become a magistrate was only appointed on New Year's Eve 1919!

- The **Human Rights Act 1998** was actually introduced in October 2000. It protects British citizens and allows them to use British courts for human rights issues.

Web activity

The Lord Chancellor's Department is a key government department that coordinates and administers the court system. Visit the website at www.open.gov.uk/lcd/ and make a list of the key functions of the department.

2 The duties and powers of lay magistrates

Duties of magistrates

Lay magistrates normally spend between 26 and 35 half-days per year hearing cases in the Magistrates' Court. Lay magistrates are unpaid except for expenses such as travel and subsistence. Two or three magistrates sit on the **bench** to hear a case. Their chief duties are:

- Dealing with summary offences. These are minor offences which can only be heard in the Magistrates' Court. They include criminal damage cases worth less than £5000 and the majority of minor driving offences.

- Dealing with either way offences/triable either way offences. These are cases which can be heard in the Magistrates' or in the Crown Court. If agreement is reached, the magistrate will hear the case. These offences are often crimes like theft or burglary.

- Passing indictable cases to higher courts: these are the most serious cases, which are therefore beyond the sentencing powers of the Magistrates' system. They include cases such as murder, rape and grievous bodily harm.

- Deciding **bail** conditions for defendants and the issuing of arrest warrants.

- Hearing youth and family cases in special separate courts: magistrates receive additional training for these important areas of their work.

- Granting licences for the sale of alcohol and the staging of entertainment events.

As magistrates are not legally qualified, the Clerk of the Court assists them. The Clerk often has a diploma in magisterial law and is there to give guidance on matters of law, court procedure and practice. However, the magistrates, rather than the clerk, are solely responsible for deciding the facts of the case and the sentencing of the defendant.

Magistrates are entitled to time off work to perform their duties, although some employers are not always supportive. Loss of earnings allowances are paid if the magistrate loses money from sitting on the bench.

In addition to lay people, the Magistrates' Courts also use District Judges. These judges are legally qualified and paid a salary; they used to be called *stipendiary magistrates*. There are only about one hundred professional magistrates in the country, half of whom sit in London courts. They hear more complex and difficult cases.

The magistrates

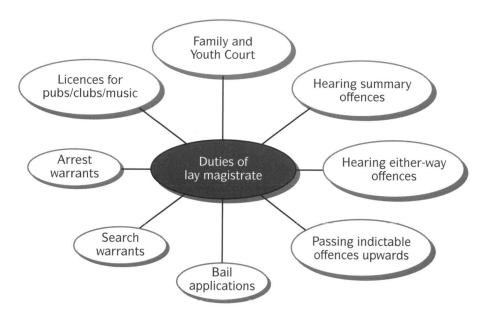

The duties of a lay magistrate

Powers of magistrates

When magistrates hear summary offences they have the following powers at their disposal:

- imprisonment
- suspended sentence
- detention in a young offenders' institute
- **absolute discharge**
- **conditional discharge**
- a fine
- an order to pay compensation
- probation order
- community punishment order
- combination order
- curfew order
- drug abstinence order
- hospital order
- guardianship order
- bail pending further reports or information.

Magistrates refer more serious cases, which are beyond their **sentencing powers**, upwards to the Crown Court.

3 Evaluation of the magistrates' system and reform

Strengths of the magistrates' system

There are clear advantages to both Government and the public of using the present system of lay magistrates.

- It is cheap and fairly quick.

- It allows local participation, which gives public faith in the system.

- It has an experienced, qualified Clerk of the Court guiding the proceedings.

- It is now covered by the **Human Rights Act 1998**, which ensures fuller explanations for decisions.

- It is developing training to improve the quality of trials and decisions.

Weaknesses of the magistrates' system

There are, however, some problems with the present system.

- Magistrates tend to be from one social group, the middle class.

- Sentencing can vary considerably from one court to another.

- The quantity of work means quality of decision-making may get worse.

- Magistrates are much more likely to convict.

- Cases are not heard in as much detail as in the Crown Court.

Reform of the magistrates' system

A number of pressures and developments have led to reform and reform proposals.

- **Cost** – Consideration has already been given to reducing the rights to a jury trial in some circumstances and trying the defendant at the Magistrates' Court rather than the Crown Court. This would considerably reduce costs and may involve increasing the present sentencing powers of magistrates. Human rights groups, members of the general public and some MPs have doubts about this development.

- **The Human Rights Act 1998** – This promises to provide a fair hearing and an effective appeals procedure for all defendants. Before the passing of this act, magistrates were not forced to give reasons for their verdicts or their sentencing. This **accountability** should improve the quality of decision-making and sentencing

- **Information technology** – The Government is keen to make the justice system as cost-effective and as speedy as possible. One way might be the use of more information technology in the courts. It is unlikely that there will be videophone trials, but paperwork might be handled more effectively by computer systems.

- **Greater use of qualified and paid magistrates** – There are only approximately one hundred District Judges (*stipendiary magistrates*). Problems with the decisions of some Magistrates' Courts, particularly in the area of dubious sentencing, have led to pressure for more full-time, professional magistrates. Cost is obviously an obstacle.

- **The Auld Report**

Sir Robin Auld's Report (October 2001) makes 300 recommendations for change and improvement to the courts system. Those affecting the Magistrates' Courts include:

- transferring some cases from the Crown Court to the Magistrates' Court, reducing the defendant's right to choose where his or her case is heard

- a new court, containing two magistrates and one District Judge, to hear middle-ranking offences

- processing some cases now heard by magistrates, such as failure to pay a TV licence, by post, so that the case never comes in front of a court.

Jargon buster

Accountability means being responsible to a body or person outside of yourself. It means that you have to answer for your decisions.

Group activity

The Metropolitan Police Commissioner has recently called for all-night courts after seeing them in operation in New York City. The view is that at present courts are based around the working patterns of those involved in the administration of the system rather than around victims and defendants. Defendants and victims may want to get the case heard and out of the way sooner rather than later. Some believe, however, that late hours will cause disruption amongst solicitors, the prison service and court staff.

1 Outline the advantages and disadvantages to the various groups involved in the court system.

2 Evaluate the effectiveness of such a system in the UK.

Revision card activity

Summarize the strengths and weaknesses of the magistrates' system.

4 The selection, eligibility and duties of jury members

The second way in which an ordinary person can play a part in the legal system is by being a member of a jury.

Selection

The jury is selected at random from the electoral register to provide a cross-section of the population. There is further selection at the court itself using cards to choose twelve jurors at random from a pool of possible jury members.

Eligibility

Before a citizen can be selected as a member of a jury, they must:

● be listed on the electoral roll

● be at least eighteen years old

● have lived in the UK for five years since they were thirteen years old.

People on the electoral roll aged between 65 and 70 do not have to serve if they do not want to. People over 70 are not selected for jury service.

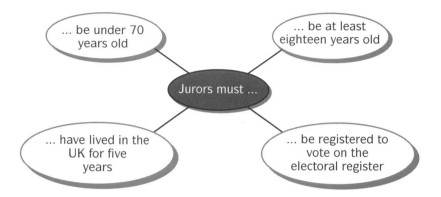

Requirements for jury service

Disqualification

Some people, on the other hand, are disqualified because of their jobs or personal circumstances. They include:

- police officers and traffic wardens

- barristers and solicitors

- people with certain mental illnesses

- anyone who has been in prison or has received a **suspended prison sentence** within the previous ten years.

Excusal

The following people have the right to refuse; they do not have serve if they do not wish to.

- MPs do not have to serve, but they can if they wish.

- Doctors do not have to serve because of the importance of their job.

- Members of the armed forces would find it almost impossible to arrange time off, so they are excused.

- People who have served within the previous two years have done their duty and are excused from jury service.

The discretion of the judge

In some individual cases, the judge will decide whether someone should serve or not. They may be asked to serve at a later date.

- Parents with young children may be excused because they would find it difficult.

- People who have pre-booked holidays may be excused by the judge.

- Students with examinations may be excused to serve at a later date.

The duties of a jury member

A jury must listen to the more serious cases dealt with by the criminal justice system. A jury member is there to listen to the evidence that is put in front of them and decide whether the defendant is guilty or not guilty.

Juries take part in criminal cases in the Crown Court and sometimes in civil cases in the County Court and High Court. The defence and prosecution will attempt to convince the jury members that their version of what happened is the truth. The jury will listen to witnesses called by the defence and prosecution. When the courtroom evidence has been heard, the jurors will withdraw to discuss the evidence and reach a verdict.

Criminal cases

These cases are heard in the Crown Court when a defendant pleads not guilty. The jury decides whether the defendant is guilty or not guilty, whilst the judge oversees the legal aspects to the case. A jury must return a unanimous verdict if it can, but if it cannot, a majority verdict of 11 to 1 or 10 to 2 will be accepted, provided the jury discusses the case for at least two hours and ten minutes. (The ten minutes was originally to cover travelling time between the jury box and the jury room.)

Civil cases

A jury is used very rarely in these cases and hears cases involving fraud, defamation of character or malicious prosecution. When a case is heard in the County Court a jury of eight is used, while the High Court requires twelve.

Jargon buster

Someone who is given a **suspended prison sentence** is not put in prison unless they commit another crime within a certain period of time.

Group activity

Do you think that the present system, with many exemptions, is the best way to select a jury? Some people have called for a system that has no exemptions. Would this give better results? Look again at the groups who are exempt, disqualified and excused.

Examination tip

Exam questions on the role of lay people will expect students to consider not only magistrates but also jurors in their answers. Be careful not to confuse who can be a magistrate with who can be a jury member.

5 | Evaluation of the jury system and reform

Strengths of the jury system

- The general public are very keen to maintain trial by jury. Ordinary people have a part to play in the system.

- Professionals have to make sure that jurors who are not legally qualified understand the proceedings. The system is kept accessible to all.

- The use of ordinary people brings the system down to earth.

- A group decision by eight or twelve people possibly gives fairer results.

- Juries have a reasonable track record for making the right decision.

Weaknesses of the jury system

- Juries may not represent a cross-section of the community.

- Jurors are not trained, apart from watching a short video and reading some leaflets.

- Some juries may find some complex cases difficult to understand.

- Jury service is compulsory, and some people may find this disagreeable.

- Verdicts do not have explanations attached, so it is difficult to see whether the case was discussed properly and fairly.

Reform of the jury system

This present system of jury trial has come under pressure for change. Society has changed, the political system has changed and even the types of offences committed have changed. Government is keen to see a cost-effective and fair system of trial with the jury as its cornerstone.

Proposals already put forward came in for fierce criticism from human rights groups and members of the legal profession. As a result, the Government commissioned the Auld Report, which took two years to produce and was published in October 2001. The Auld Report affects not only magistrates but also juries. Reform suggestions include:

- smaller juries

- fewer disqualifications and excusals

- defendants losing some rights to be tried by jury

- greater support for jury members, possibly with summaries of key facts

- overruling jury decisions and sending them to appeal where the judge felt the verdict was 'perverse'

- reducing randomness of selection to make juries reflect the community better

- telling juries of defendants' previous convictions.

The Government is now listening to the feedback the Auld Report has generated and is soon to put some of its 300 recommendations into practice.

The Auld Report – more work for magistrates, less for jurors

Group activity

Jill Dando was the popular presenter of the TV programme *Crimewatch*. She was shot dead on her doorstep after returning home from a shopping trip. After a huge police enquiry, the suspected killer was eventually arrested and taken to court. The jury found Barry George guilty of murder by a majority of 10 to 1 after many hours of discussion in the jury room. After the trial it was revealed that Mr George had a series of convictions for harassing women.

1 Do you think juries should be informed of the defendant's previous record, as the Auld Report suggests?

2 What effect would this have on the way a jury viewed a person with or without a record of previous convictions?

3 Will the jury give better or worse verdicts using this information?

Revision card activity

Summarize the points on strengths and weaknesses of the jury system.

Outline means 'give a brief sketch' and evaluate means 'give your opinion'.

Revision checklist

1   Lay people include both magistrates and jurors.

2   Lay magistrates are not paid or legally qualified but they receive training.

3   Magistrates hear 98 per cent of criminal cases; they can imprison for up to 6 months and fine up to £5000.

4   Magistrates hear summary offences, have the option to hear either way offences but send indictable offences to the Crown Court.

5   There is continuing concern about the unrepresentative social class of magistrates.

6   Jurors may not really be a representative sample of the electorate because of excusals and disqualifications.

7   Juries may find some cases very complex.

8   General public has faith in jury system but is often not keen to participate.

9   Government is keen to cut the cost of jury trials but human rights groups oppose changes.

10   Auld Report will affect role of lay people by weakening power of juries and strengthening power of magistrates.

Quick revision questions

1   What are the key duties of lay magistrates?

2   Why are magistrates seen as cost-effective?

3   Who selects magistrates and what is looked for in them?

4   What kind of training do magistrates receive?

5   What are the strengths and weaknesses of the magistrates' system?

6   What are the key roles for a member of a jury?

7   How are jury members selected?

8   Name two proposals for jury reform.

9   Who is eligible and ineligible to become a jury member?

10   How is the Auld Report going to affect juries and magistrates?

Exam question

1 *a* Outline the key elements in the selection of jury members. (15 marks)

   b Evaluate possible ways of achieving a more representative jury. (15 marks)

Exam answer guide

1 *a* Jurors are selected from the electoral register. They must be 18 or over and have lived in the UK for five years since the age of thirteen. Some people are not allowed to be a juror or can gain exemption. They include:

✓ excusals

✓ disqualifications

✓ judge's discretion

b The number of excusals may make the modern jury unrepresentative. Some say that employed middle-class people escape their duty, leaving the jury with more than its fair share of housewives, retired people and the unemployed. Points that you could also make include:

✓ Auld Report and relevant changes

✓ possibility of no excusals or disqualifications

✓ problems with altering present system

✓ problems with achieving a 'true representation'.

Unit 2

The legal profession – barristers, solicitors and legal executives

Key points

1 The training, roles and promotion of barristers
2 The training, work and promotion of solicitors
3 Roles of Bar Council, Law Society and Ombudsman
4 The training, work and promotion of legal executives

What do I need to know about the legal profession?

The world of barristers, solicitors and legal executives is undergoing huge changes. You will need to know the main provisions of the **Court and Legal Services Act 1990** and the **Access to Justice Act 1999** in order to answer questions effectively. These two pieces of legislation have laid the foundation for change. You must understand the selection, training and work of the legal profession against the background of the legal revolution taking place.

The barristers

1 | The training, roles and promotion of barristers

There are approximately 10 000 barristers working in England and Wales. The organization responsible for the training and discipline of barristers is called the Bar Council. Unusually, the Bar Council also deals with complaints about barristers. There has been criticism of this system and as a result the Government is looking at a more independent complaints body. Much of this change has come via provisions made in the **Court and Legal Services Act 1990**.

Training

Route number 1 to becoming a barrister

1 Law degree.

2 Bar Vocational Course. This is a one-year course organized and monitored by the Bar Council, focusing on skills needed when the law student becomes a barrister.

3 Pupils join one of the four Inns of Court in London. This is an opportunity to meet, socialize with and make connections with more experienced barristers.

4 The student is then called to the Bar, which means they are qualified as a barrister.

5 Before they can appear in court, however, they must find a place to become a pupil to an experienced barrister. This involves two separate sixth-month periods and is called *pupillage*. Normally for the first six months the pupil barrister shadows a barrister, and during the next six months may represent clients in court.

The training of barristers

Route number 2 to becoming a barrister

1. Student has a degree in a subject other than law.

2. Common Professional Examination: this is a one-year conversion course that covers key parts of a law degree.

3. Steps 2–5 of route number 1.

The work of barristers

You may have been on a visit to see a Crown Court or seen barristers at work in television programmes such as *Kavanagh QC* and *Judge John Deed*. Their main duties are:

- acting as advocates for clients in the Crown Court

- preparing 'opinion', which is their view on legal issues, for clients. They are often asked whether a case is worth pursuing.

- preparing pre-trial paperwork to make sure that the case they are working on is processed as efficiently as possible.

Once they qualify, barristers are normally self-employed. They are not allowed to form partnerships, but they work together with other barristers in a workplace called *chambers*. The barristers share the building, a clerk and other running expenses. The clerk arranges the business of the chambers, allocates the cases and often negotiates the fees charged for work.

Obstacles for newly qualified barristers

The financial realities of a barrister's life can cause problems. Many students leave undergraduate degree courses with considerable debt. Student barristers have to cope with the added financial burden of the Bar Vocational Course and a year as a pupil. For those without wealthy backgrounds the early days can be a real struggle. Fees are normally a long time in coming to the newly established barrister. The effect of this is that many new members of the profession leave before they become established.

The work of barristers

Promotion of barristers

A barrister who has been working for ten years can apply to become a Queen's Counsel (QC). This is an honorary title much cherished by barristers. It is awarded by the Lord Chancellor to the best junior barristers in the country. All barristers are called junior barristers until they are made Queen's Counsel.

There are many advantages to being a QC. Social status is enhanced, and in their professional role QCs can charge more and receive more interesting and important cases.

The final stage in the life of a barrister may be elevation to the judiciary. Although judges are well paid, some barristers may have to take a pay cut to become a judge, but the status is usually compensation enough.

Did you know?

When a barrister is made a QC, it is called 'taking silk' because they exchange their ordinary cotton robe for one made of silk.

Quick question

What are the two main routes to becoming a barrister?

Newly qualified

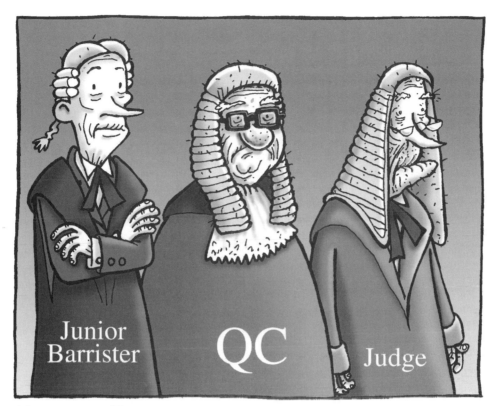

Junior Barrister

QC

Judge

The progression of barristers

Web activity

Check university websites for law schools which provide the Bar Vocational Course. Find out in more detail the areas of law covered by the courses. What skills are developed when taking such a course?

Group activity

The tremendous financial commitments involved in the training of barristers often prove impossible for many young barristers and their families to cope with. How might the legal profession and their clients lose out from such a state of affairs?

Revision card activity

Using index cards note the key points on the training, work and promotion of barristers

Examination tip

Good time management in the exam will give you a better grade. Comments on your answer paper such as 'I ran out of time' do not impress examiners.

2 The training, work and promotion of solicitors

Most people who need legal advice or legal work done start with the services of a solicitor. There are approximately 80 000 solicitors in England and Wales.

Training

Solicitors have the same type of training as a barrister in the initial phase, but then go on to specialize. The training consists of:

1 Academic stage: a degree in law or any degree plus a Common Professional Examination/Postgraduate Diploma in Law.

2 A one-year course called the Legal Practice Course (LPC).

3 Two years of practical on-the-job training, including a Professional Skills Course which lasts 20 days.

4 Enrolment with the Law Society. The student is now a solicitor.

5 Ongoing training while working as a solicitor.

The work of solicitors

Solicitors' work includes:

● acting as advocates in the Magistrates' Courts

● drawing up and processing last wills and testaments

The training of solicitors

The work of solicitors

- divorce proceedings

- working on issues concerning tax

- the production of commercial contracts

- conveyancing (the legal process of buying and selling property).

A solicitor may work in a solicitor's practice or eventually run their own business. About 15 per cent of solicitors seek employment outside the private sector, working with local authorities, the Crown Prosecution Service, Government departments, etc.

The work of solicitors is varied, and the very strict separation between what solicitors and barristers do in the legal world is gradually breaking down. The **Court and Legal Services Act 1990** has slowly begun to change the strict division between the work of solicitors and barristers. Increasingly, solicitors may be seen in higher courts representing clients. Solicitors need an Advocacy Certificate to work in the Crown Court and above. It is still to be seen whether solicitors with this certificate get the same opportunities for work in the judiciary.

Legal case: Hall v Simons (2000)

This case clarified the legal position of solicitors who were sued by their clients. Their immunity from prosecution seems to have been lifted in all areas. Prior to this case, solicitors and barristers could not be sued for their work as advocates since it was felt that clients might blame the skills of the lawyer rather than the nature of the case, which might have been very difficult for anyone to win.

Revision card activity

Note the key points on the training, work and promotion of solicitors.

The solicitor

Examination tip

Knowledge of recent changes to the work of legal professionals will impress examiners. Note the **Court and Legal Services Act 1990** and the **Access to Justice Act 1999**.

3 Roles of Bar Council, Law Society and Ombudsman

Bar Council

The Bar Council oversees the training, work and discipline of barristers. It is a powerful self-regulating organization, which makes up its own rules and it very defensive of its members. Change is something it prefers to ignore.

Law Society

Solicitors also have a professional body called the Law Society. It supports solicitors but also uses a disciplinary procedure if there are any complaints made by the public against a solicitor. It oversees training and provides a number of support services. The Law Society, like the Bar Council, is coming under pressure to change and modernize.

Legal Services Ombudsman

The Legal Service Ombudsman (LSO) investigates the way complaints about either barristers or solicitors are dealt with. The LSO system is not designed as an appeal process. If there is a belief, however, that the original complaint was not dealt with properly, the LSO will ask the Bar Council or Law Society to review the matter. The LSO is keen to see that the disciplinary body arrived at a decision that was reasonable.

The Legal Service Ombudsman was established as part of the **Court and Legal Services Act 1990**. The full power of the Ombudsman has yet to be felt. The Government hopes that self-regulation will eventually work, but it is felt by many that time is running out for the current disciplinary procedures.

Other changes to the world of solicitors and barristers

In addition to the many changes to the professions pushed through by the Government, other developments are also taking place:

Competition from supermarket locations

Competition may soon come from firms who take the law to the shopper. Law outlets are being planned for shopping centres and other High Street and community locations.

Telephone advice 0898 style

Some solicitors operate from premium-rate telephone lines advertised in local newspapers. No demand for payment is made, apart from an inflated phone bill. Clearly this is an effective way to start a relationship with a potential client.

Internet advice

Internet law advice is on the increase in the United States, and it is probably only a matter of time before it develops in the UK. It may be difficult to hold the adviser to account if things go wrong, but it may be cheaper for straightforward legal tips.

Claims direct

The 'no win no fee' system introduced as the result of changes to the Legal Aid scheme has encouraged a number of companies to drum up business for solicitor's firms by large-scale TV promotions and handing out leaflets in the High Street.

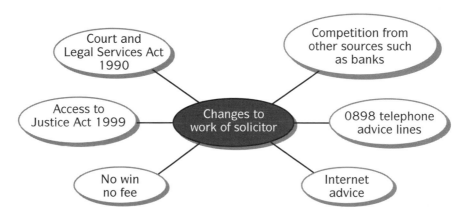

Changes to the way solicitors work

Web activities

1 Investigate the Bar Council, at www.barcouncil.org.uk. What services does it offer to barristers? What key issues is it struggling with at the moment?

2 Find the Law Society's website at www.lawsociety.org.uk. Investigate the aims of the Law Society, the services it offers and the current issues is it attempting to resolve.

3 Go to the website for the Legal Services Ombudsman at www.olso.org and find out why this service exists. Why is the Government keen to encourage its use?

4 Explore the Institute of Legal Executives website at www.ilex.org.uk. Gather further information about the career routes open to members of ILEX and the personal qualities that they are expected to possess.

4 The training, work and promotion of legal executives

Role of paralegals

Paralegals work in the world of law, but in a support role to solicitors and barristers. There is a Paralegal Association which represents their interests, but this is not as firmly established or as well known as the bigger group – legal executives.

Legal executives

Legal executives are the biggest and most important group of non-professional but legally qualified workers. They work alongside barristers or solicitors. There are around 23 000 legal executives.

Training of legal executives

Legal executives work while they train. If they join straight from school they can expect to earn £8–9000 per year. After they are fully qualified they can expect to earn £20–24 000 per year.

They have to take courses and examinations organized by their professional body, The Institute of Legal Executives (ILEX). The training is a combination of self-study, evening courses and day-release. The employer often helps with the cost of the course.

There are three main steps to becoming a fully qualified legal executive.

1 Student: a series of courses covering areas encountered in the legal profession, i.e. family law, civil disputes, criminal cases and conveyancing.

2 Membership: students apply for enrolment after completing parts 1 and 2 of their membership qualification.

3 Fellowship: for full admission, candidates must be at least 25 years old and have five years' experience in a legal office.

Work of legal executives

The day-to-day work of a legal executive is very similar to that of a solicitor. Legal executives can often find themselves in the front line when dealing with clients. They go to court to support solicitors and may be asked to attend police stations to gather information from clients who are being held in custody.

Supervision of legal executives

Legal executives are supervised by their own professional body called the Institute of Legal Executives (ILEX). They have a very flexible career and training structure which can lead to fully qualified legal status as a solicitor.

Revision checklist

1. There are approximately 10 000 barristers in the English legal system who are supported, trained and disciplined by their association, the Bar Council.
2. Training for barristers includes: Law degree (or Common Professional Examination), Bar Vocational Course, and one year as a pupil barrister.
3. There are approximately 80 000 solicitors in the English legal system who are supported, trained and disciplined by their association, the Law Society.
4. Training for solicitors includes: Degree in Law (or Common Professional Examination/Postgraduate Diploma in Law), Legal Practice Course, two years of on-the-job training (including 20-day Professional Skills Course).
5. Work of barristers involves: acting as advocates, normally in the Crown Court; preparing opinions for clients; and pre-trial paperwork.
6. After ten years, barristers may become Queen's Counsel, which is an honorary title signifying excellence awarded by the Lord Chancellor.
7. Work of solicitors involves: acting as advocate, normally in the Magistrates' Court, working on last wills and testaments and probate, divorce proceedings and commercial work, such as tax and contracts.
8. Solicitors may act as advocates if they possess a Certificate of Advocacy.
9. Paralegals work alongside solicitors and barristers. Biggest branch is legal executives.
10. Legal Services Ombudsman investigates poor service on behalf of the public.

Institute of legal executives

Revision questions

1 Outline the routes to becoming a barrister.

2 Outline the routes to becoming a solicitor.

3 What are the key functions of a barrister?

4 What are the key functions of a solicitor?

5 What is a Queen's Counsel?

6 Name a key aim of the **Court and Legal Services Act 1990**.

7 What does the Bar Council do?

8 What does the Law Society do?

9 What are the main duties of legal executives?

10 Which Act of Parliament created the Legal Services Ombudsman?

Exam question

1 *a* Outline the main training stages of solicitors and barristers. (10 marks)

   b What are the criticisms of the present system of training? (20 marks)

Exam answer guide

1 *a* The main training stages are:

   ✓ Academic – the degree course

   ✓ Vocational – the BVC or the LPC

   ✓ Professional – two-year training contract for solicitors and the pupillage for a barrister.

   Outline in brief what each of these stages consists of.

   b Criticisms are about equal opportunities and access for the less well-off.

   ✓ BVC is very expensive

   ✓ Little financial support for a pupil barrister

   ✓ Training contracts very difficult to get; it might be useful if they already know someone in the system

   ✓ Training can take many years, which means huge debts for ordinary students.

   Result may be a very elitist legal profession. Barristers may not understand or be able to communicate effectively with the clients they hope to serve. Good-quality potential barrister candidates who do not have the necessary financial background may be lost.

Unit 3

The judges

Key points

1 The key functions of judges

2 The main types of judges and where they are found

3 The selection, appointment and training of judges

4 The role of the Lord Chancellor

5 The independence of the judges and their dismissal

Why do I need to know about judges?

Essay questions on this subject will require students to know not only the part played by judges in the legal system but also how independent they are of the politicians who employ them. Independence of the judiciary is a complex legal and political situation. For insight into the thinking of the Government, it would be wise for students to get a clear understanding of the **Human Rights Act 1998**. In theory this piece of legislation gives judges even more independence than they already have. This is one of the most

The judiciary

important changes to affect the English legal system for many centuries. You should be prepared to quote any relevant articles and assess the act's impact when tackling essays on this subject.

1 The key functions of judges

When judges are talked about as a group they are known as the *judiciary*. They are found in a variety of settings in the English legal system, in both civil and criminal courts. Their key functions are:

- overseeing the conduct and procedures of the trial

- acting as the legal expert when it comes to points of law

- in criminal cases, summing up the case, informing the jury of the relevant law and delivering a sentence if the jury finds the defendant guilty

- in civil cases, deciding on the facts of the case and, when no jury is sitting, the verdict, as well as the **remedy** for the injured party.

Judicial Review

One of the most important functions of the judge is that of Judicial Review, which is carried out in the Queen's Bench Division of the High Court. The Judicial Review examines the legality of a decision made by a court, by a public organization, such as a local authority, government or by any other large organization, such as the Football Association. The Judicial Review can overturn the decision if it finds that the decision:

- involved an error of law

- was so unreasonable that no reasonable authority would have taken it

- went against natural justice.

The court will only act when there is no other option for appeal available.

The Human Rights Act 1998

The **Human Rights Act 1998** came into force in the English legal system in October 2001. From that date the provisions of the act were part of English law and had to be interpreted and applied by English judges.

There are fourteen main articles to the act, but the following may be of particular significance to the judiciary:

- The right to a fair public and independent trial

- Freedom from laws which did not apply at the time of the 'offence'

- The right to an effective solution to a human rights issue

- Freedom from discrimination.

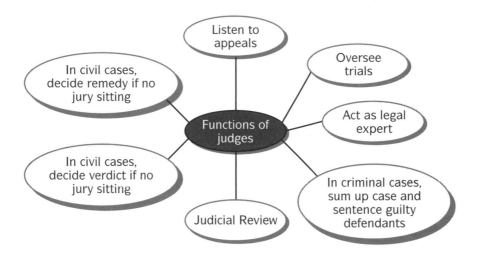

The functions of judges

Jargon buster

Remedy is the compensation or damages offered to the person who has suffered a wrong in a civil case.

Examination tip

Find out the key provisions and more details about the **Human Rights Act 1998** on www.hmso.gov.uk/acts/acts1998/19980042. Answers that include reference to the **Human Rights Act** will stand out.

2 The main types of judges and where they are found

Judges below High Court level are known as *inferior judges* and those at and above High Court level are known as *superior judges*. Magistrates are not part of the judiciary, though they may carry out some similar duties. Magistrates are not legally qualified and only work part-time. We will look at the different judges in order of increasing power.

Inferior judges

District Judges (Magistrates' Courts)

This is a new type of judge born out of the **Access to Justice Act 1999**. They were previously known as *stipendiary magistrates*. They sit in the Magistrates' Courts and hear cases alone. Despite sitting in the Magistrates' Court, District Judges (Magistrates'

Courts) are fully legally qualified and have at least seven years' experience as a solicitor or barrister. They are also, unlike lay magistrates, full-time and fully paid.

The District and Deputy District Judges

These judges hear civil cases in the County Court. These judges normally listen to small claims cases. They are qualified solicitors or barristers with at least seven years' experience.

Recorders and Assistant Recorders

Recorders and Assistant Recorders are part-time judges who sit in the Crown Court and the County Court. The rest of their time is spent practising as either solicitors or barristers. The job is on a fixed-term contract, normally for three years. At the end of this time, either side can pull out. The job is used to see whether the person is suitable and willing to carry out the duties of a judge.

Circuit Judges

These judges listen to more complex civil cases in the County Court. They may also be found in the Crown Court. They are either chosen from barristers and solicitors with at least ten years' experience or from existing Recorders and District Judges.

Superior judges

High Court Judges

High Court Judges are chosen from barristers or solicitors with at least ten years' experience or from those who have been Circuit Judges or academic lawyers. Applications can now be made by individuals since the **Court and Legal Services Act**, but the Lord Chancellor still reserves the right to appoint the person he thinks is the best candidate. High Court Judges sit in one of three courts:

- The High Court (Chancery, Queen's Bench and Family)
- The Crown Court, to listen to very serious cases
- The Divisional Courts, to hear appeals.

Lord Justices of Appeal

These judges sit in the Court of Appeal and are selected from those who have had rights of audience in the High Court for ten years or from existing High Court Judges.

Lords of Appeal in Ordinary (the Law Lords)

These judges sit in the House of Lords and are selected from those judges who have held senior judicial posts.

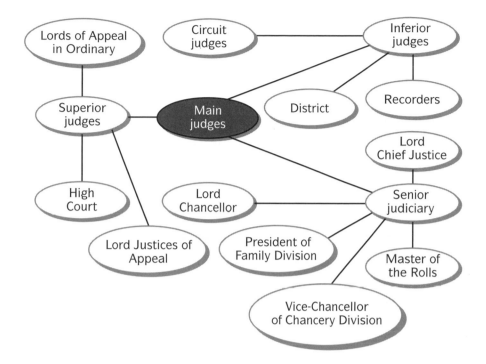

The main types of judges

Senior judiciary

The senior judiciary comprises:

- the President of the Family Division of the High Court

- the Vice-Chancellor, who manages the Chancery Division

- the Master of the Rolls, head of the Civil Division of the Court of Appeal

- the Lord Chief Justice, head of the Criminal Division of the Court of Appeal

- the Lord Chancellor, who is a senior member of the Government and effectively in charge of the English courts system. This brings some problems about conflict of interest. The Lord Chancellor is also officially head of the Chancery Division.

Quick question

What is the Auld Report?

Revision card activity

Using index cards, construct a set of cards showing the key details of the judges and where they are to be found.

1   There are proposals from the Auld Report, which looked at the efficiency of the entire court system, to produce a new type of court that will have a District Judge (Magistrates' Courts) sitting with two lay magistrates to hear middle-ranking criminal cases. Seek out the Lord Chancellor's website on www.open.gov.uk/lcd/ for details of this ground-breaking report. What are the key aims of this report? What resistance will these recommendations face, and from where?

2   Go to the Lord Chancellor's website at www.lcd.gov.uk and collect more information about judges. Salaries are public information and are listed on this site. How do these salaries compare with those of senior barristers and solicitors?

3   Go to www.open.gov.uk/lcd/judicial/judgesfr.htm to find out the names of the current senior judiciary. It might be useful to know the key figures when reading news items about developments in the legal system.

3   The selection, appointment and training of judges

Selection and appointment

The Lord Chancellor plays a crucial role in the appointment of all judges.

Inferior judges

Inferior judges are those below High Court level. They are Circuit Judges, Recorders and Assistant Recorders, District Judges and District Judges (Magistrates' Courts) or Stipendiary Magistrates. The **Court and Legal Services Act 1990** has brought some important changes for the appointment of these judges. Posts are now advertised and potential candidates apply for interview. The Lord Chancellor still has the final say, however.

Superior judges

Superior judges are those of High Court level and above. They comprise the Law Lords, the Lord Justices of Appeal and High Court Judges. The Lord Chancellor's Department carries out most of the work of selection. It collects information on suitable people and then approaches them to see if they want the job. This may involve the **old boy's network** and possibly corrupts the process of selection.

Senior judiciary

The senior judiciary are the most important posts in the legal system. They are: the Lord Chief Justice, the Master of the Rolls, the President of the Family Division and the Vice-Chancellor of the Chancery Division. The Lord Chancellor puts names forward, in order of preference, to the Prime Minister. The Prime Minister normally accepts the guidance of the Lord Chancellor on these matters.

The training of judges

The Judicial Studies Board is the formal organization that provides judges with their initial training and keeps them up to date with legal developments affecting their work. The judges are of course qualified barristers or solicitors, but it has been said that the duties of judges are very different from the experience gained as advocates. The key training consists of a one-week residential course for newly appointed judges, followed up by refresher courses.

Jargon buster

The **old boys' network** involves friends or relatives helping each other to get jobs or promotion. This may disadvantage candidates who do not have such connections.

Did you know?

Although lay magistrates are not part of the judiciary, the Lord Chancellor also has the power of appointment over them. After interview, the local Advisory Committee puts names forward for consideration, but the Lord Chancellor has the final say as to whether a person is chosen.

Web activity

Find out more details on the work and training of judges at the Judicial Studies Board at www.cix.co.uk/~jsb/index.htm. What do you think of the training offered? Are there any improvements that you could suggest?

Examination tip

Use revision cards to help you remember difficult terms. Look for relationships within the work you are revising. Draw up a diagram showing the network of judges.

4 The role of the Lord Chancellor

The Lord Chancellor acts as a link between three important parts of the legal-political system. He is:

- a member of the Cabinet, which means he plays a part at the heart of Government in a political capacity

- a member of the parliamentary process in the House of Lords, so that he is involved in the legislative process

- Head of the Chancery Division of the High Court, which means that he plays an important judicial role.

The Lord Chancellor has a major part to play in the appointment of inferior and superior judges, and the Lord Chancellor's Department is a key Government institution. The Lord Chancellor is appointed by the Prime Minister and therefore often has strong personal and professional links to the heart of Government. The role is a strange one in a system that often has checks and balances to prevent the possibility of corruption and conflict of interest.

The Theory of Separation of Powers

Montesquieu was a French philosopher who believed that powers in a state should be separate. The power should be held in three areas so that no one area became too powerful:

- The *executive*, in other words the Government that proposes the law

- The *legislative*, meaning the Parliament that makes the law

- The *judicial*, that is, the judges, who see that the law is fairly enforced.

Our Lord Chancellor is present in all three of these areas. He is a member of Cabinet (the Government), he is a member of the House of Lords (the Parliament) and he is in theory head of the Chancery Division of the High Court (the judiciary).

The Lord Chancellor

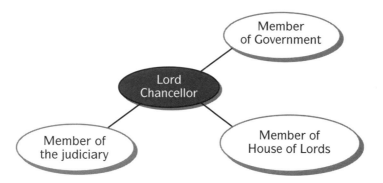

The roles of the Lord Chancellor

Quick question

Would the system run more or less effectively with a separation of powers as suggested by Montesquieu?

Group activity

There have been recent calls for the abolition of the job of Lord Chancellor. Do you agree, or is it important to have one person with an overview of the legal and political system? Is the present system the most effective method of selecting judges? What other procedures might be possible in the selection of judges?

5 The independence of the judges and their dismissal

Judges are clearly open to pressure from a variety of sources.

- The Government may wish to hear one verdict rather than another on important cases that affect its own policies and budgets. A recent ruling on the status of refugees in the UK may leave the Government open to huge compensation payments for illegal imprisonment. One must bear in mind, however, that the Lord Chancellor appoints senior judges in the first place.

- Multinational companies and other lobbying groups can exert huge financial and political pressures on judges. Judges must be free to make decisions on their interpretation of the facts and legal position. As part of this, however, they must be independent from any self-interest.

- The general public supported by tabloid newspapers can sometimes attempt to persuade judges to change their rulings on controversial and sensitive cases. The judges' independence gives them a firm foundation to resist such attention. Judges have immunity from being sued on judicial decisions.

- The media in all its shapes and forms can try to influence the outcome of cases.

Legal case: R v Pinochet (1998)

General Pinochet, the former Chilean dictator, was held for extradition by the UK Government. One of the judges, Lord Hoffman, was seen as having an outside interest in the case through his association with human rights group Amnesty International.

Tenure

The word *tenure* refers to how secure a person's job is and how long it is to last for. Judges have very secure tenure because of the nature of their job. Judges must be in a position to know that the decisions they make will not result in them losing their job.

Dismissal

The dismissal of judges is very difficult. The system prides itself on having independence from pressures that might be put upon it by Government, the general public or other sources, therefore judges need to feel secure in their posts.

Judges of the High Court and above (superior judges) are covered by the **Act of Settlement 1700**, which means that a judge can only be dismissed if both Houses of Parliament petition the Queen to do so. The last time this happened was in 1830.

Independence of the judges

Judges below High Court status (inferior judges) can be dismissed by the Lord Chancellor using the **Courts Act 1971**. Again, this power is rarely used. For those judges on fixed-term appointments, the Lord Chancellor may choose not to extend the contract. In reality, the Lord Chancellor 'persuades' judges to retire or resign if he thinks they should not continue in their posts, rather than using formal procedures to remove them.

In addition to dismissal, The Lord Chancellor may remove a judge who has a permanent disability that means they cannot perform their duties.

Group activity

The vast majority of judges have come from public schools, from wealthy backgrounds, are white, middle-aged and older, and male. Given the background of judges, can they be independent and fair in their decision-making?

Revision checklist

1 The Lord Chancellor plays an important part in all judicial appointments. Up to Circuit Judge level is by application and interviews, above this the Lord Chancellor approaches and suggests candidates.

2 Judges below High Court are called *inferior judges*. High Court Judges and above are called *superior judges*.

3 The Judicial Studies Board is responsible for the training of judges.

4 *Tenure* refers to job security. Dismissal of judges is difficult. Normally judges are persuaded to 'retire' rather than sacked.

5 Judges need to be independent and must resist pressure from Government, powerful companies, the public and the media.

6 The main roles of judges are: conducting trials, acting as legal experts, summing up and sentencing in criminal cases and giving the verdict and awarding damages in civil cases.

7 Judicial Review involves judges reviewing decisions made by lower courts and large public or private organizations.

8 The main types of judges are: District, Circuit, High Court and Appeal Judges.

9 The Lord Chancellor is a powerful political and legal figure who is seen in the Government, the Parliament and the judiciary.

10 The French Philosopher Montesquieu thought it best to separate the three areas of power: the executive (Government), the legislative (Parliament) and the judicial (the judges).

Quick revision questions

1 What changes did the Court and Legal Service Act bring to the appointment of judges?

2 Who appoints the most senior judges?

3 What is the role of the Judicial Studies board?

4 How can judges be dismissed?

5 Where might pressure on judges come from?

6 What are the key duties of a judge?

7 What does the Judicial Review do?

8 What articles of the **Human Rights Act 1998** most apply to the work of judges?

9 List the main types of judges in the English legal system.

10 Why would Montesquieu worry about the Lord Chancellor?

Exam question

1 *a* How are judges selected for their posts? (15 marks)

 b What are the main criticisms of how judges are selected? (15 marks)

Exam answer guide

1 *a* Judges are selected in different ways, depending on how high up the pecking order they are:

 ✓ Up to Circuit Judge level by advertisement, application and interview. Lord Chancellor can still in theory appoint his own choice.

 ✓ Above circuit judge level, Lord Chancellor's Department collects information on suitable candidates and reports back to the Lord Chancellor. Candidates are approached and, if interested, appointed.

 ✓ For very senior judges the Lord Chancellor suggests likely candidates to the Prime Minister. The suggestions are put in order of preference. The Prime Minister can choose to ignore advice but normally follows the lead of the Lord Chancellor.

 b Not so bad for judges lower down the pile, but for more senior posts the process is secret and may be very unfair. Equal opportunities issues arise, as does the influence of the old boys' network. The information collected by the Lord Chancellor's Department may be inaccurate and biased. Some say the influence and the power of the Lord Chancellor over appointments is too great.

Unit 4

The finance of legal services

Key points

1 Methods of financing legal advice and representation
2 Unmet legal need and the **Access to Justice Act 1999**
3 The new bodies created
4 Strengths and weaknesses of the present system

Why do I need to know about the finance of legal services?

Questions on this subject will ask you about methods of financing legal advice and the problems individuals often have when doing so. Clearly the Government has played a significant role since the 1950s in providing funding for less well-off individuals. You need to know about the impact of the latest system of state funding resulting from the **Access to Justice Act 1999**. Questions will invite you to comment on the fairness and justice of the work of the Legal Services Commission and its two subsidiaries. Questions in this area will expect you to have views on how successful the changes have been. You will need to understand the structure of the new system, why it was introduced and its effectiveness.

Access to justice

Methods of financing legal advice and representation

There are many ways of funding or obtaining legal advice and representation in addition to private purchase.

Household insurance policies

As part of the package protecting householders' possessions, there is often a clause offering some element of legal insurance. A great many people are covered, but the numbers who realize this or use this service may be much smaller.

Legal insurance

Specific legal insurance is quite common in other countries and may become more common in the United Kingdom if the trend towards more frequent use of the legal system continues.

Trade unions

Trade unions often retain a solicitor's firm to give advice on employment issues such as contracts. Most also have a facility which offers advice to its members on other issues.

Citizens Advice Bureaux (CAB)

The Citizens Advice Bureaux provide a very popular free advice service which people are often happy to approach and use. There are close to 2000 branches around the country. There are, however, two problems facing the CAB. First, their popularity puts a great strain on the resources available. Second, the resources available are inadequate for most of the branches. They are victims of their own success, and also demonstrate the huge demand for legal services that are convenient, informal and free of charge.

Law centres

Although there are only about 50 law centres, they face the same problems as the CAB, with huge demand and insufficient resources. Their popularity, along with the CAB, underlines the need for free and informal systems of advice. Law centres are normally set up in poorer areas to reduce the problem of unmet legal need amongst more disadvantaged social and economic groups.

Independent advice offices

There are close to a thousand small, independent legal advice centres covering areas such as welfare benefits, housing issues and debt advice. Often these are funded by churches, housing associations and charities.

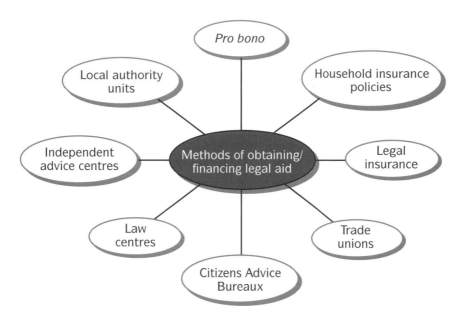

Methods of obtaining or financing legal advice

Local authority units

Some local authorities provide free legal advice on a range of areas, including housing and social security benefits. They may also include a trading standards office, which can provide expert advice in consumer protection.

Pro bono

Pro bono means that free legal advice and representation are provided to needy individuals by private law firms. *Pro bono* first gained prominence in the United States but the practice is growing in popularity in the UK, helped by both the Law Society and the Bar Council.

There are also a variety of political and media pressures to make the vocabulary of law simpler so that 'ordinary people' can understand what was going on in the legal system. More use of Alternative Dispute Resolution (ADR) is also being encouraged, to reduce costs and make the legal process less formal.

Web activity

Get onto the site of the Citizens Advice Bureaux at www.nacab.org.uk and select information on the range of services available at the CAB.

Did you know?

The Benson Commission 1979 looked at the provision offered and suggested that the CAB was a crucial part of the network which should perhaps get increases in Government funding to improve access to justice.

Examination tip

Always brainstorm a short plan for a good answer.

2 Unmet legal need and the Access to Justice Act 1999

Since 1949 the allocation and administration of state-funded legal advice and representation had been the responsibility of the Legal Aid Board. The Legal Aid Board had gradually become less efficient, and major financial and operational problems had begun to emerge. There were three key reasons for this.

1 Costs were becoming greater and greater. The number of people being helped, however, was in some years actually going down. The Government feared that unscrupulous lawyers were 'milking the system'.

2 Unmet legal need was not being cured. One of the main objectives of the Legal Aid Board was to ensure that those who needed support would get it. Even after fifty years, this was still a long way off.

3 Legal aid provision was unevenly provided between different Magistrates' Courts, and guidelines were not followed properly for the merit testing of cases. Access to justice was clearly being denied to some defendants.

The **Access to Justice Act 1999** introduced a coordinating body called the Legal Services Commission, which oversaw two new legal bodies: the Community Legal Service and the Criminal Defence Fund. This important piece of legislation fundamentally reformed access to Government-funded legal services for poorer members of society. It also brought some major changes to the legal profession – it allowed solicitors to speak in higher courts such as the Crown Court if they had the appropriate training and qualification. The qualification was called an Advocacy Certificate.

Many people who might benefit from legal advice and representation do not, however, receive it. Some reasons for this situation have been identified. People may:

● not understand that they may benefit from a legal process

● not be able to find a convenient service to help them

- not be able to afford the service

- lack awareness of state-funded legal support or conditional fee arrangements

- lack the confidence to mount a legal action or even approach a solicitor

- overestimate the true cost of legal services

- have family or work commitments which prevent the pursuance of a case.

Did you know?

A discussion document, called a White Paper, had come before the **Access to Justice Act 1999**. It was called *Modernising Justice*.

Web activity

For further information on the **Access to Justice Act 1999**, see the website at www.open.gov.uk/lcd and look for the section headed 'Access to Justice'.

Group activity

Contact a local solicitor and see if they will give you information on the areas of law they practise in and how much typical cases cost. Possibly one letter or phone call per group would avoid overstretching the solicitor's secretary!

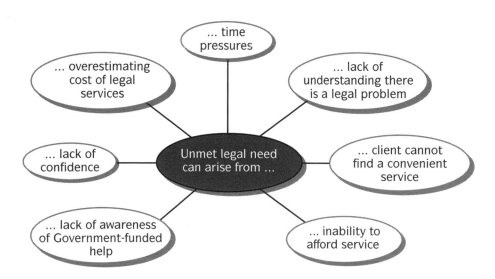

Causes of unmet legal need

The Legal Services Commission

The Legal Services Commission came into being on 1 April 2000. It replaced the old Legal Aid Board which had done the job for nearly 50 years. The Commission aims to meet the Government's objectives, which are:

'to promote and develop legal services that can be delivered within a controlled budget and to target them according to need'.

The Legal Services Commission makes contracts with providers of legal advice. The number of solicitors will only be around 5000, which is a significant reduction on numbers under the old system.

Community Legal Service

The Community Legal Service (CLS) now handles civil cases. It has a number of functions including:

- coordinating the set budget through its regional offices, although there is a central fund for particularly expensive cases

- targeting funds at the most deserving cases

The Legal Services Commission

- providing general information about the legal system
- providing support in resolving disputes.

Funding criteria

The funding of cases relies on a set of criteria laid down by the Government for the CLS to use. They include:

- cost versus benefit
- money left in the CLS fund
- importance to the public interest
- importance to the individual
- alternatives available to the individual
- the part the individual played in the case itself.

Contracts

From January 2001 organizations that wish to provide Government-funded legal services for civil cases must have a contract to do so from the CLS.

Conditional fee/no win no fee arrangements

There has, however, been one other important change that affects many people seeking legal advice. From 1 April 2000, the vast majority of personal injury cases are subject to 'no win no fee' arrangements. These are also known as *conditional fee* arrangements. Cases which fall outside 'no win no fee' are subject to a new funding code which gives priority to housing cases and those cases that involve a wider public interest.

Exclusions from funding criteria

There are also a number of other exclusions from the system put in place by the funding criteria:

- conveyancing (the buying and selling of houses)
- last wills and testaments
- trusts (ways of avoiding tax on your wealth and income)
- company law and other business issues
- libel (written lies about a person) and slander (spoken lies about a person).

The Criminal Defence Service

The Criminal Defence Service is the second body under the control of the Legal Service Commission. Its aims are to:

'Secure advice, assistance and representation to those involved in criminal investigations or proceedings.'

No win no fee

Under this service a duty solicitor is available free of charge to a person who is being detained or questioned by the police. This advice is sometimes only available via the telephone.

At the court, a duty solicitor will advise defendants, again free of charge. They may also represent a person in court when there is an emergency situation. This may be when an application for bail is being made.

In general Criminal Defence Service assistance is available to anyone who needs advice in the interests of justice and can meet the financial tests laid down.

Priority

The funding criteria for both civil and criminal legal aid ensure that the criminal service takes priority. Criminal cases are the most serious court cases and often involve situations where a defendant could lose his or her liberty by being put in prison. If a regional Criminal Defence Service fund runs out of money due to unexpected demand, resources are automatically diverted from civil into criminal.

 ## Quick question

What are the criteria for funding a case?

Group activity

We are all expected to obey the law. Should the Government therefore target publicly funded legal services or should everyone get support when they have a legal problem?

Web activity

Find the CLS website on www.justask.org.uk. This site illustrates some of the support available to people with legal problems.

Revision card activity

Summarize the work of the Legal Services Commission, the Community Legal Service and the Criminal Defence Service.

4 Strengths and weaknesses of the present system

There have been winners and losers as a result of the fundamental shake-up in the legal aid system. These include legal service providers as well as clients.

Strengths of the present system

- Funding is targeted to the more deserving cases via the funding criteria.

- Information is more readily available to those who need legal advice via leaflets and the Internet.

The strengths of the present system of Government-funded services

- Community Legal Service is planning partnerships with other national and local bodies to improve legal advice coordination.

- There is more consideration of mediation and negotiation services rather than resorting to a formal court hearing.

- Conditional fee arrangements may encourage more people to seek a legal solution to an injury or accident.

The weaknesses of the present system

- Conditional fees may be more difficult to arrange if you have a weaker case, and it is argued access to justice may therefore be reduced.

- Fees may be high in relation to damages won.

- Some may find it difficult to meet the funding criteria needed in civil cases.

- It may be difficult to attract the best calibre of lawyer, given the pressure put on fees by Government spending limits.

- The quality of lawyers may deteriorate in the public system as payments for state-funded legal work lag behind those in the private sector.

- Contracting of lawyers would reduce the array of available legal advisers and could unfairly affect small, ethnic-minority practices.

Revision card activity

Using index cards, summarize the strengths and weaknesses of the present Government-funded legal advice system.

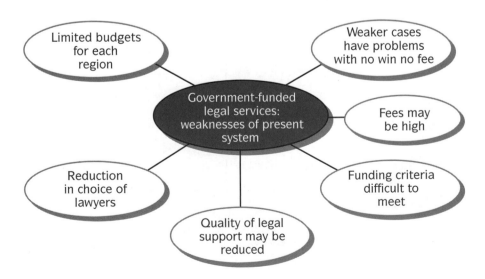

Weaknesses of the present system of Government-funded legal services

Revision checklist

1 Legal advice can be obtained in the following ways: private purchase insurance policies, trade union provision, Citizens Advice Bureaux and Law Centres, Local Authority Provision and *pro bono*.

2 Unmet legal need exists because of lack of knowledge, lack of suitable service, cost, and pressures of work and family life.

3 **Access to Justice Act 1999** created three new bodies to administer Government funding and advice on legal matters: The Legal Services Commission, The Community Legal Service and The Criminal Defence Service.

4 The Legal Services Commission coordinates Government funding of legal services and attempts to coordinate legal providers.

5 The Community Legal Service deals with civil cases and manages a budget which is shared between various regions around the country.

6 The Criminal Defence Service deals with criminal cases. It provides duty solicitors at police stations and at Magistrates' Courts. It takes priority when there is a shortage of funding.

7 Funding criteria exist to allocate available funds to where Government thinks they should be targeted.

8 An important part of the new structure is the widespread use of conditional fee arrangements, known as 'no win no fee', for personal injury claims.

9 Conditional fee arrangements allow the solicitor to charge the client for the cost of a normal case and then add a success fee to the total.

10 Some solicitors put a cap on the total charged so that clients do not see their damages swallowed by fees if those damages are low

Quick revision questions

1 List six ways of financing or obtaining legal advice.

2 What is unmet legal need?

3 Name three reasons for the existence of unmet legal need.

4 What are the main duties of the Legal Services Commission?

5 What are the main aims of the Community Legal Service?

6 Why does the Community Legal Service have to use funding criteria?

7 What are conditional fee arrangements?

8 Name two benefits and two drawbacks of conditional fee arrangements.

9 What does the Criminal Defence Fund do?

10 Name two advantages and disadvantages of the present provision of legal services by the Government.

Exam question

1 *a* What types of cases are funded by the Government? (10 marks)

b What are the key problems with 'no win no fee' cases? (20 marks)

Exam answer guide

1 *a* The Government has decided to prioritize its funding of cases. Criminal cases, which may result in the defendant going to jail, are seen as more important. Civil cases are now mostly dealt with by conditional fee arrangements, so the work is put onto the shoulders of the client and the risk onto the solicitors.

b No win no fee' cases create problems for both client and solicitor.

For the client:

✓ May find it difficult to find a solicitor if their case is weak

✓ Solicitors may talk up the problems and increase their success fee

✓ Fewer providers under the new scheme.

For the solicitor:

✓ They get no payment if they lose the case

✓ May have to do unpaid work examining cases they end up not taking

✓ May be forced to cap fees at too low a level.

The clear winners are the Government. They now have a system which has cut public spending and possibly still improved access to legal services overall.

The criminal courts

Why do I need to know about the criminal courts?

Examination questions will expect you to know the functions and workings of the two main criminal courts, the Magistrates' Court and the Crown Court. The criminal courts judge some of the most serious criminal offences. You need to understand the appeal process and the reasons for the creation and the role of the Criminal Cases Review Commission. The *Auld Report* will have a major impact on the workings of the

The criminal system

Criminal Court system. Students need to be aware of the proposals and the effects of the *Auld Report*.

1 Pre-trial matters

Between the offence and the criminal trial there are many stages. The police play their part investigating, the Crown Prosecution Service (CPS) considers whether to go ahead with prosecution, and the courts themselves have to go through their own pre-trial procedures. These processes are designed to reduce unnecessary costly trial proceedings and prevent people who should not be in front of a court from appearing there. The overall structure is known as the **Criminal Justice System**.

The role of the police

The police have an investigative role when an offence is committed. They collect evidence from the scene of the crime, interview prosecution witnesses, arrest and question the suspect, and charge them if they feel they have sufficient evidence. Many people who are charged are later found to be innocent. The charge allows the police more time to conduct their investigations and indicates to the accused the direction of the case and the possible need for legal advice.

Minor offences are often dealt with by a *caution*. A caution is a warning to the offender to mend his or her ways. A record is kept of cautions given by the police. A caution can only be given, however, if the offender admits to being guilty and is prepared to accept the caution in good faith. Most cases of drunk and disorderly are dealt with by a caution when the offender sobers up, normally the next morning. Cautions are now also going to be the norm for the possession of cannabis, rather than a court appearance before the magistrates.

Cautions are particularly effective with children. The **Crime and Disorder Act 1998**, which has a number of provisions affecting young people, strengthened the cautionary element (now called *warning and reprimand*) with regard to children in the hope of keeping them out of court and out of the Criminal Justice System completely.

The Crown Prosecution Service

The Crown Prosecution Service (CPS) was created by the **Prosecution of Offences Act 1985**. Once the police have gathered evidence on the offence, the case is passed to the Crown Prosecution Service. The CPS has to decide whether to proceed with the case or drop it. Its main function is to prosecute offenders on behalf of the state, but it will only prosecute a case if there is enough evidence and the case is in the public interest.

The CPS has been criticized for dropping too many cases before they come to trial. This criticism came from victims and their families, and also from two reviews examining the work of the CPS: the Glidewell Report 1998 and the Narey Review 1997. As a result of these pressures the CPS was restructured and now has 42 regional centres rather than one central office. It also has more liaison with local police forces. It was hoped that users would find the CPS service more accessible and more understanding.

The main functions of the CPS are:

- reviewing evidence to assess the chance of prosecution success

- giving guidance on the evidence that is submitted by the police

- prosecuting cases in the Magistrates' Courts

- hiring (known as *instructing*) qualified advocates to prosecute cases in the Crown Court.

The role of the courts pre-trial

The courts are clearly interested in reducing the number of cases they have to hear. There are a number of costs involved in every court case:

- financial cost of professional legal advice

- taxpayer's costs in running the Criminal Justice System

- the emotional cost to victims, defendants and their families

- costs of custodial sentences if the case goes to conviction and sentencing

- time taken in calling witnesses and jurors.

There are a number of ways that the Criminal Justice System (CJS) filters cases out. We have already looked at two: the initial investigation by the police and the assessment of the Crown Prosecution Service on whether to proceed. The courts also play their part.

Every criminal case starts at the Magistrates' Court and, depending whether it is summary, triable either way or indictable, it remains at the first level or moves up to the Crown Court.

Summary offences are the most minor cases and are dealt with relatively quickly. A summons is sent to the accused, who is asked to appear in front of the Magistrates' Court at a specified time. If a guilty plea is lodged, a summary of the facts is read to the court. The defence solicitor may make a statement explaining any background facts relevant to the defendant's actions. The statement by the defence solicitor is known as a *plea in mitigation*. This may shape the magistrates' sentencing of the defendant.

Offences either way are those which can be heard before a Magistrates' Court or a Crown Court. The defendant appears before the magistrates and is asked whether they plead guilty or not guilty. If there is sufficient evidence for a Crown Court trial, a **prima facie** case is said to exist and the case is committed to the Crown Court. These are known as *committal proceedings*. This is a way the magistrates can filter out cases which should not go further up the system to the Crown Court.

The defence will try to prove that no case exists if they want the case to be heard in the Magistrates' Court or be dismissed completely. The magistrates will read the evidence that is produced against the accused and make a decision. If they feel that there is no case to answer, the defendant will be free to go. If more evidence is gathered at a later stage, the process may start all over again and the accused may be sent to the Crown Court for trial by jury.

Indictable offences are the most serious of all criminal cases. They are now quickly transferred to the Crown Court by order of the **Crime and Disorder Act 1998**. The court will then hear evidence and the plea of the defendant and decide whether there is a case to answer. This process of identifying the key aspects of the case is known as a *plea and directions hearing*. If the defendant pleads guilty, a judge will hear the case and decide sentence. If the defendant pleads not guilty, the case will go before a jury who will listen to the facts and produce a verdict. If guilty, the judge sentences the defendant. If the jury has decided a verdict of not guilty, the defendant is discharged.

The procedure is designed to protect suspects from unnecessary court proceedings and ensure that the most expensive court practice does not try trivial cases.

Jargon buster

- The **Criminal Justice System** includes prisons, the Probation Service, the courts and the Crown Prosecution Service.

- The **Crime and Disorder Act 1998** was a key piece of legislation from the new Labour Government. It hoped that its promise to be 'tough on crime and tough on the causes of crime' would be met in some part by this piece of legislation.

- The prosecution has to prove to the magistrates that the case is serious enough for the Crown Court. If they are successful, a ***prima facie*** case exists. In other words, there seems to be enough evidence to go further.

Examination tip

Read the question on the criminal courts carefully and answer all its aspects.

2 Bail

At any point after being arrested by the police, the accused can apply for bail. If bail is granted, the accused person is free to go but promises to return at a later point to a police station or a court. The police or the court can offer bail. The **Bail Act 1976** indicates a 'presumption' that the person will receive bail.

Reasons for bail

The criminal process can be long and bureaucratic. There are witness statements to be taken, court records to be completed, solicitors may have to talk to barristers or seek other advice, and the court itself may not have a convenient free date for many weeks,

The Bail Act 1976

if not months. Even when a defendant has been found guilty, there may be
pre-sentence reports to be completed to give those sentencing a better picture of the
defendant's background. What should be done with the accused in the meantime? The
presumption in English law is that the defendant is innocent until proved guilty. Even
if guilty, the defendant may not receive a custodial sentence if there are extenuating
circumstances. It would be very unfair to hold an innocent person in jail awaiting the
chance of the prosecution to prove them guilty. The answer to this dilemma is bail.

Refusal of bail

Unless there are good reasons for refusal, **The Bail Act 1976** presumes that bail will be
granted. Reasons for denial include:

- suspicion that the accused would fail to return as promised

- suspicion that the accused would commit further offences while they were free
  on bail

- suspicion that the accused would interfere with the course of the criminal enquiry
  or intimidate potential court witnesses

- fear that the accused might be intimidated, injured or killed if released on bail

- the defendant has no secure address (although **bail hostels** can be used in these
  cases).

Conditions associated with bail

Bail is often offered with conditions.

- The defendant may be ordered not to approach or communicate with the victim or even not to go into the local area where the victim of the alleged crime lives.

- The accused person may have to report daily or weekly to a police station to prove they have not absconded or they may even have their passport confiscated to prevent escape overseas.

- An electronic tag may be worn around the ankle to let the authorities know where the defendant is.

Sureties

If it is feared that a person may not return after being bailed, the court may ask for some form of security. A person who is prepared to pay the court a sum of money if the accused fails to return is known as a *surety*. The amount of money required for this guarantee depends on:

- the crime itself

- the quality of evidence against the accused

- the character of the accused

- whether the accused ever abused the bail process before.

If a defendant does not turn up when asked to, the surety pays the money agreed. It is not paid in advance. This is different from many other countries which demand money before the defendant is released. A recent case, involving some British plane spotters who were arrested in Greece on spying charges, highlighted the differences. Each of the accused had to pay £9000 before they were released on bail.

The prosecution may use **The Bail (Amendment) Act 1993** to appeal against the award of bail if they consider there are reasons that the accused will prove unreliable and fail to appear later. This is normally in cases where the maximum penalty is five years or more. It is felt that the longer the possible imprisonment, the greater the chance of the accused not returning.

There is a problem here of balancing the needs of the two sides. The criminal court system wants to process offenders and the general public want to be protected against potentially dangerous offenders. The offenders, however, want to retain their right to freedom until a court of law proves them guilty. Many people **held on remand** are later found not guilty or receive such short prison sentences that they are immediately released from custody. The courts therefore have to be careful in balancing up the rights of each party.

- **Bail hostels** offer the chance for homeless people to be given bail. They provide a secure address where the accused must live and can be contacted.

- Prisoners **held on remand** are not guilty and are entitled to their own food and their own clothes. They also have more generous mail, telephone call and visitor rights than other prisoners.

3 Mode of trial

The Magistrates' Court plays a vital part in deciding the mode of trial relevant for each offence. At the moment the defendant has a degree of choice in either way offences, although proposals from the Auld Report may reduce this choice. For the convenience of the system, cases are classified into one of three categories: summary, either way or indictable. The first are heard in the Magistrates' Court, the second either in the Magistrates' Court or the Crown Court, and the third only in the Crown Court.

Magistrates' trial

Trials in the Magistrates' Court are relatively quick. They involve:

- reading out a summary of the facts
- seeking a plea of guilty or not guilty from the accused
- arguments put forward by prosecution and defence
- a verdict from the magistrates if there has been a plea of not guilty
- sentencing or a request for further information to help with sentencing
- release if not guilty.

Crown Court trial

The Crown Court process is a little more involved. It consists of the following steps:

1   Prosecution lawyers outline their case against the defendant.

2   Prosecution witnesses are called to give evidence against the defendant.

3   The defence **cross-examines** the prosecution evidence.

4   Defence lawyers outline their case in support of the defendant.

5   Defence witnesses are called to support the defendant.

6   Prosecution lawyers cross-examine the defence evidence.

7   The prosecution, defence and judge **sum up** the case.

8   The jury is brought to a private room where they can speak to no one about the

case. They have to reach a verdict based on the evidence. The verdict should be unanimous, but if they cannot do this within two hours and 10 minutes the judge may accept an eleven to one or a ten to two majority.

9 If the defendant is found guilty, the defence make a case for leniency before sentencing by the judge.

10 If the defendant is found not guilty, he or she is free to leave the court.

Jargon buster

- **Cross-examination** is the process of questioning witnesses to test their evidence. It is an essential part of the adversarial court system we use.

- **Summing up** means that each side puts their version of the evidence to the jury. The judge tries to summarize the evidence and events impartially to help the jury reach a verdict and will also raise any relevant points of law.

Group activity

Double jeopardy means that a defendant who is found not guilty cannot be tried for that same offence again, even if more evidence appears at a later stage that possibly proves their guilt. The Government is thinking of taking this right away.

1 Do you think double jeopardy should be abandoned in the interests of justice?

2 Why do you think such a rule exists?

4 | Committal proceedings

Committal proceedings move triable either way cases from the Magistrates' Court to the Crown Court after the magistrates have listened to the case against the defendant. The law covering committal proceedings is contained in the **Magistrates Courts Act 1980**.

Section 6 (1) of the **Magistrates Courts Act 1980** requires all prosecution evidence to be read and considered by the magistrates before they consider whether there is a case to answer at the Crown Court.

According to Section 6 (2) of the act, the defendant is automatically referred to the Crown Court with the permission of the defence lawyer. In this case the magistrates do not formally consider the evidence.

More finely balanced cases will probably be subject to Section 6 (1) treatment. If the CPS indicates that this is a relatively serious 'either way' offence, Section 6 (2) tends to be used.

Committal proceedings

Jurisdictions of Magistrates', Youth and Crown Courts

Magistrates' Court Jurisdiction

The word *jurisdiction* means the power the court has to deal with a particular legal matter. Some powers of jurisdiction overlap between courts. For example, either way offences can be heard in the Magistrates' Court or the Crown Court.

Magistrates have jurisdiction over all minor criminal cases (summary cases) and those either way offences where it is decided they should be heard in the Magistrates' Court. They also have jurisdiction over some civil matters. Look back at Unit 1 of Module 1 for further information.

The Magistrates' Court is the first port of call for all criminal offences. It acts as a filter for the Crown Court, preventing unsuitable cases going forward, and tries 98 per cent of criminal cases. It deals with two types of cases:

 Summary cases involving custodial sentences of up to six months (or twelve months if two offences are heard together) or a fine of up to £5000.

 Triable either way cases if it is decided that they will be heard in the Magistrates' rather than the Crown Court.

The **Magistrates' Court** hears all cases and sends serious indictable offences to the Crown Court. This is known as *mode of trial proceedings* and the details are about to change as a direct result of the Auld Report. Many more cases will be heard in the Magistrates' Courts and 'middling offences' may now be heard in a new type of court, with one district judge and two magistrates.

Other functions relating to the criminal element of Magistrates' Court work include:

● hearing bail applications

● issuing arrest warrants to the police

● issuing search warrants to the police.

Youth Court jurisdiction

The Youth Court has jurisdiction over most criminal cases involving young people aged between ten and seventeen. It is part of the Magistrates' Court and is staffed by lay magistrates who have specialized training. Very serious criminal charges such as murder and manslaughter are dealt with in the Crown Court. A young person may also appear in an adult court if they are charged as a co-defendant with an adult.

The proceedings in the Youth Court are less formal than in other criminal courts. Parents or guardians of offenders under sixteen must attend the hearings unless there are very exceptional circumstances. The court has the power to order attendance by parents or guardians. Press reporting is restricted and there is no public gallery. The bench must have at least one female and one male magistrate.

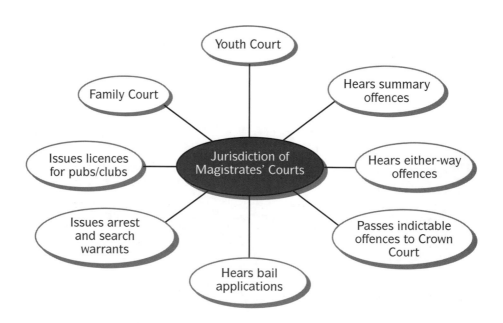

The jurisdiction of Magistrates' Courts

Crown Court jurisdiction

The Crown Court has jurisdiction over indictable criminal cases or either way offences referred up from the Magistrates' Court. It deals with the most serious criminal offences and also hears appeals from the Magistrates' Court. Circuit Judges or Recorders staff the court.

6 Appeals

An appeal is a challenge to a decision made by a court. The convicted defendant may be able to lodge an appeal against conviction or sentence. In some cases the prosecution may lodge an appeal if they believe the sentence handed down to the defendant is inadequate or that a point of law needs clarification. Once a person is acquitted, there can be no appeal against this decision under double jeopardy rules.

There are three important concepts that are relevant when examining decisions made by courts and deciding whether an appeal is relevant. Each is described by a Latin phrase:

- *Audi alterum partem* – both sides should be heard

- *Nemo judex in causa sua* – no one should be allowed to judge their own case

- *Ultra vires* – no organization should act beyond its powers.

An appeal against sentence by the prosecution is actually dealt with officially by the Attorney General under the **Criminal Justice Act 1988**. The Court of Appeal may agree to increase the sentence, leave it the same or even decrease it.

Appeal from a trial of a summary offence

There are two main ways an appeal from a Magistrates' Court is dealt with.

An appeal from a summary trial conducted in a Magistrates' Court is normally to the Crown Court. A judge will sit with two magistrates to hear the appeal. The Crown Court may vary the sentence or can pass the case back to the Magistrates' Court for further consideration. The Crown Court will normally give an opinion to guide the magistrates.

An appeal can also be made to the Queen's Bench Divisional Court to get advice on a point of law or of legal procedure. The case can go to the House of Lords if there is no solution at this level. The prosecution or defence can use this route for appeal.

Appeal from a trial of an indictable offence

There are two possible types of appeal from the Crown Court.

An appeal can be made to the Court of Appeal (Criminal Division). The appeal can consider whether the conviction is unsafe. The Court of Appeal can also consider the sentence and vary this if appropriate.

Alternatively, an appeal can go to the House of Lords if, in the opinion of the Court of Appeal, a general point of law is raised through the case. The case can only go to the House of Lords if either the Court of Appeal or the House of Lords is of the opinion that this is the best place to find a solution.

7 The role of the Criminal Cases Review Commission

In response to pressure from a number of sources, the Government established an independent body, the Criminal Cases Review Commission (CCRC), to consider possible miscarriages of justice. The cases of the Birmingham Six and the Guildford Four had brought the system in disrepute in some people's eyes. The **Home Secretary** had previously been responsible for reviews and referrals to the Court of Appeal, but it was felt that the political nature of the post might affect the outcome when high-profile cases were inspected. The CCRC is substantially free from Government pressure. It can query convictions and sentences and ask for the case to go back to court.

The main functions of the CCRC are:

- to consider suspected miscarriages of justice

- to arrange investigations of the case if appropriate

- to refer cases to the Court of Appeal if there are grounds uncovered by the investigation of the case

- to settle outstanding issues on request from the Court of Appeal

- to refer cases to the Home Secretary for consideration of Royal Pardon

- to give advice to the Home Secretary when he or she is considering a Royal Pardon.

The CCRC has a huge workload and insufficient resources to deal with the task. Whether a case is taken up and processed is very much a matter of luck. Justice is served by having the CCRC, but at a very slow pace.

Jargon buster

The Home Secretary is one of the most senior politicians and is responsible for law and order issues and the police service.

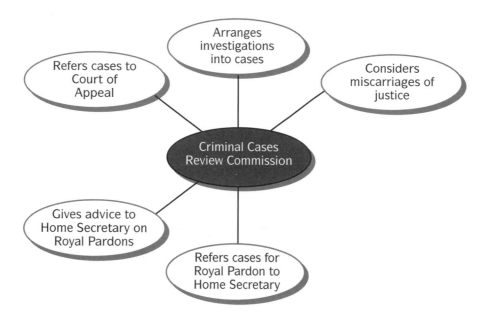

The Criminal Cases Review Commission

 Did you know?

The Birmingham Six and the Guildford Four were innocent men accused and convicted of terrible bomb outrages during the 1970s. Pressure for convictions led to serious miscarriages of justice in these cases. All the men were subsequently released (except for one who died in prison).

 Web activity

Look up www.ccrc.gov.uk and identify the key functions of the CCRC and the reasons for its creation.

Revision checklist

1 The police investigate the offence and pass papers to the Crown Prosecution Service, who decide whether to prosecute or not.

2 Cautions are used by the police to warn offenders not to repeat their behaviour.

3 All criminal cases start in the Magistrates' Court. All summary and some either way offences are heard there too.

4 More serious offences are sent to Crown Court. They are known as *indictable offences*.

5 Bail is covered by the **Bail Act 1976** and allows people to go free if they agree to come back to court or to a police station in the future.

6 Jurisdiction, meaning the cases courts hear and their power:
- The Magistrates' Court hears more minor offences, known as summary offences, and some triable either way cases
- The Youth Courts deal with people aged ten to seventeen
- The Crown Court deals with the most serious criminal cases called indictable offences.

7 Appeals involve challenging the decision of a court. Appeals can be made against sentence, conviction or point of law.

8 Appeal from a summary offence in the Magistrates' Courts goes to the Crown Court or the Queen's Bench Division of the High Court.

9 Appeal from an indictable offence in the Crown Court goes to Court of Appeal (Criminal Division), or to the House of Lords on a point of law.

10 The Criminal Cases Review Commission looks into possible miscarriages of justice, arranges investigation of cases if necessary, and refers cases for appeal or pardon.

Quick revision questions

1 What is the role of the police in a criminal case?

2 What is a caution?

3 What is the main function of the Crown Prosecution Service?

4 What are grounds for refusing bail?

5 How is a case tried in a Magistrates' Court?

6 How is a case tried in the Crown Court?

7 What are committal proceedings?

8 What does the word *jurisdiction* mean?

9 How does the appeal system work?

10 What specific cases led to the creation of the Criminal Cases Review Commission?

Exam question

1 *a* Outline the main steps in a criminal trial. (15 marks)

   b Evaluate the need for an effective appeals procedure in the criminal courts system. (15 marks)

Exam answer guide

1 *a* Outline means 'give a brief description of'. Points to include:

   ✓ Committal proceedings

   ✓ Plea and directions hearing

   ✓ Prosecution outlines case

   ✓ Witnesses called for prosecution

   ✓ Cross-examination

   ✓ Defence do the same as above

   ✓ Everyone sums up

   ✓ Jury returns a verdict and judge sentences.

   b Appeals procedure is needed because:

   ✓ Miscarriages of justice take place

   ✓ Witnesses can be unreliable

   ✓ Sentences are custodial

   ✓ Jury or judge may make mistakes

   ✓ Prosecution or defence may not do their job properly

   ✓ Public need faith in the system

   ✓ Defendants must have a fair deal.

The system of law and order is very important to ordinary citizens and society. It must be fair and seen to be fair. Mistakes can be made, so an appeals procedure shows the system is big enough to admit error quickly and effectively. The key word to look out for here is 'evaluate'. This means giving your opinion based on your analysis of the issues. This is where you can gain high marks.

Unit 6 · The civil courts

Why do I need to know about the civil courts?

Civil law is about trying to solve disputes between various people and various organizations. A full understanding of the civil court system and the areas that connect to it will provide you with a useful insight into your syllabus. Questions on the civil courts will expect you to know about the structure, power and appeal routes available. Insight and comments on recent reforms would also be invaluable. The Woolf Review

Civil disputes

of the Civil Court System 1996 is one of the most significant. Also covered in this unit is the tracking system used in the civil courts and information on the work of the County Court and the High Court. This is an important area of your AS course to know well since it has so many links to other parts of your syllabus.

1 The County Court

The County Courts came into existence in 1846 in order to provide a system of accessible local courts. There are around 220 County Courts in the United Kingdom. The process of using the County Court is fairly cheap and relatively straightforward. The County Courts deal with a wide range of civil cases and have been a success overall. Most people who have to use them consider the process effective and fair.

The process used in the civil courts is laid out in the **Civil Procedures Rules 1999**. These rules were an attempt to update court procedures and simplify and update some of the language used in court. These are also known as the Woolf Reforms after Lord Woolf. The aims of the rules are to:

- ensure both sides are treated fairly, irrespective of their power

- deal with cases according to their importance

- persuade both sides to reveal all relevant facts they hold on the case

- encourage an agreement before or even during a court hearing if possible.

2 Small claims track, fast track and multi-track cases

Pressure exerted by the Consumers' Association led to a new method of dealing with small civil cases. It was felt that the County Court did not represent the interests of less well-off **claimants**. People were often discouraged by fears of cost and complexity. To answer these criticisms, the **small claims** procedure was created. Recent reforms by Lord Woolf have refined the system further. Cases are sorted into one of three categories called *tracks*. It is hoped that by dealing with cases in this way, delays can be avoided and the cases can be heard more quickly.

Small claims track

Cases involving sums of money under £5000 are heard in the small claims track. The small claims track is a *method* of conducting a case. The case is heard in an ordinary courtroom in the County Court. Appeals are now allowed from the small claims track since the introduction of the **Human Rights Act 1998**.

The small claims track procedure:

- is less formal than many other court hearings

Small, fast and multi-track

- gets to the truth by asking penetrating questions (**inquisitional** methods) rather than by more aggressive methods

- has a limit on total costs because claimants and defendants are encouraged to represent themselves rather than seek professional legal representation

- does not allow the winning side to claim costs

- has a District Judge to hear the case.

Fast track system

This procedure covers cases that involve sums of money between £5000 and £15 000. Both sides of the dispute see information about the case and the witnesses before the start of the trial. Fast track cases are normally heard within a day. Costs are capped to reduce the financial burden on the **parties** involved, and cases are heard within 30 weeks of being allocated to the fast track. If fast track cases are particularly complex they may go upwards to the next level, which is called the multi-track system. The vast majority of cases involving the ordinary public are covered by the small claims track and the fast track system.

Multi-track system

These are the most expensive cases heard in the County Court and cover disputes which involve sums of money over £15 000. If cases are particularly

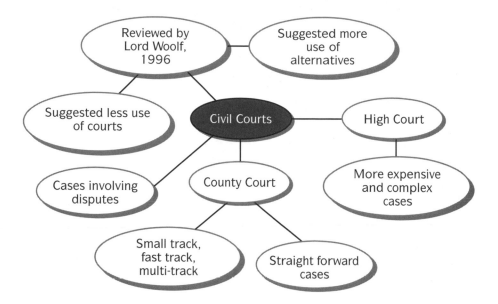

The civil courts

time-consuming they may be heard in the multi-track system to allow more time for a solution.

Jargon buster

- **Adversarial** methods of getting to the truth involve rather aggressive and vigorous asking of questions. **Inquisitorial** methods try to uncover the issues by more gentle but thorough questions.

- The word **claimant** is used for someone who starts a civil case. The word **plaintiff** was used before new **Civil Procedure Rules** were brought into force in April 1999, and is still often used.

- The different sides involved in a case are called **parties**.

Did you know?

The small claims process can be activated by a phone call to the nearest county court. The claimant can request a pack of information and an application form.

Research activity

County Courts are open to the public and are often attached to the local Crown Court. Try to visit and see both courts in operation. Identify the key differences between the two.

Web activity

The Consumers' Association is a campaigning pressure group which seeks changes in the law to benefit consumers. Locate their site at www.consumersassociation.org and identify their current legal campaigns.

Group activity

'Inquisitorial processes attempt to get to the truth whilst adversarial processes attempt to win.'

These two approaches may produce different evidence and outcomes. Should the following areas of civil court work be adversarial or inquisitorial? Give reasons for your answers.

1 Disputes between people who owe each other money.

2 Some divorce cases and custody of children.

3 Disputes between landlords and their tenants.

4 Settling the financial affairs of people who have died (probate).

5 Personal injury cases.

6 Cases relating to the **Race Relations Act 1976**.

Examination tip

Only do what the question asks, no more, no less.

3 The High Court

The High Court deals with civil cases. Its headquarters are in London and are known as the Royal Courts of Justice. There are also 24 regional High Courts around the country. The High Court deals with the more complex cases. It is divided into three divisions which specialize in different types of case.

The Chancery Division deals with business disputes, companies that become insolvent, and copyright disputes (when one side claims another is stealing its business or intellectual ideas). The Chancery Division is headed by the Lord Chancellor, although because of his huge workload the Vice-Chancellor does most of the work. This division has eighteen High Court Judges hearing cases.

The Queen's Bench Division hears cases involving contract disputes, debt, personal injuries and **tort**. It is the largest of the divisions of the High Court and has 70 High

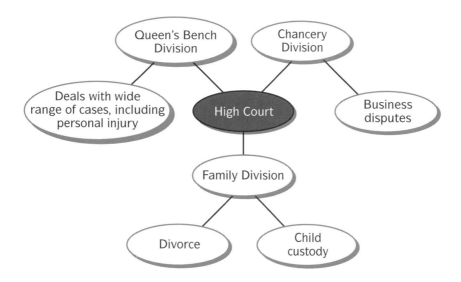

The High Court

The hierarchy of the civil courts

Court Judges, headed by the Lord Chief Justice. It is also used for Judicial Review, which happens when judges review decisions taken by public bodies or other large organizations.

The Family Division was created in 1970. It hears difficult or complex divorce cases and also makes judgments about the custody of children. It is headed by the President and has seventeen judges.

The High Court normally has a single judge hearing cases, but the Queen's Bench Division may have a civil jury in defamation cases. In these cases the jury listens to the facts and decides the amount of compensation that is paid to the claimant. Appeals from the High Court are made to the Court of Appeal.

Jargon buster

- **Tort** is a French word meaning 'a wrong'. Claimants take cases to court to obtain compensation to make up for the wrong done to them.

- **Defamation** means ruining a person's reputation by telling lies about their character.

4 Jurisdiction of the courts

The term *jurisdiction* means the work of each court or the power of that court to deal with a case. *Original jurisdiction* refers to where the case was first heard.

Unlike cases in the criminal system, which all start in the most junior court, civil cases can start at any point. The civil system is not straightforward. The claimant may have a case which involves a relatively small sum of money but has extremely complex legal arguments attached. On the other hand, a case may have a great deal of money involved but a relatively straightforward legal argument attached. It can be a problem deciding which level of the civil court system to start in.

A number of different courts may claim that it is within their power to hear a case. The court with the most day to day power is the High Court. Recent reviews mean that County Courts can now hear cases with a much higher monetary value, which increases the jurisdiction overlap between the various civil courts.

Courts, cases and judges

Whose case?

Jurisdiction of the Magistrates' Court

Magistrates' jurisdiction on civil matters includes:

- hearing disputes over Council Tax payments
- hearing family cases at the Family Court
- licensing pubs and clubs to sell alcohol
- licensing musical and other entertainment events
- issuing betting and gaming licences.

Jurisdiction of the County Court

The County Court hears a wide range of cases including:

- disputes between people who owe each other money
- uncontested and straightforward divorce cases
- hearings exploring the custody of children
- disputes between landlords and their tenants
- settling the financial affairs of people who have died (probate)
- personal injury cases
- cases involving the **Race Relations Act 1976**.

Jurisdiction of the High Court

The three divisions of the High Court deal with some of the most important and complex civil cases.

The Chancery Court handles:

- copyright disputes covering theft of ideas and inventions
- claims on trusts, wills and business partnerships
- bankruptcy proceedings
- difficult probate cases.

The Queen's Bench Division hears:

- contract cases
- negligence cases
- personal injury cases.

The Family Division has jurisdiction over:

- divorce cases
- child custody cases.

One of the main problems facing the successful claimant in a civil case is collecting the award they may be given. The Civil Court has no power to order the loser to pay up unless the winner of the case begins another case against them. This next stage known as *enforcement proceedings* and may involve:

- obtaining money directly from the employer of the person who owes the money, using the **Attachment of Earnings Act 1971**
- getting a warrant to take away goods owned by the person, possibly using professionals known as *bailiffs*
- taking money directly from a bank account or savings account by obtaining a *Garnishee Order*
- bankruptcy proceedings if the person owes more than £750; this will affect their ability to obtain credit and run a business.

Examination tip

Spider graphs will help you see relationships and make learning easier.

The compensation

5 | Appeals and appellate courts

Appeals in the civil court system normally involve moving up to the next most senior judge. There are, however, courts that hear nothing but appeals from other courts. In civil cases there are circumstances where both sides can appeal on either the award made by the court or on the facts of the case and the points of law which arose during the trial.

Appeals from the County Court

- In a small claims track case, a Circuit Judge would hear an appeal of a decision taken by a District Judge.

- A fast track case heard by a District Judge would be appealed to a Circuit Judge.

- A fast track case heard by a Circuit Judge would have an appeal heard by the High Court.

- The most important civil cases heard in the County Court, the multi-track cases, go for appeal to the Court of Appeal.

Appeals from the High Court

All decisions from the High Court go to the Appeal Court (Civil Division) for an appeal hearing.

The divisions of the High Court also act as **appellate** courts, known as Divisional Courts. They hear appeals from the courts below them. The Divisional Courts correspond to the three divisions of the High Court: Chancery, Queen's Bench and Family. The most important Divisional Court is the one attached to the Queen's Bench Division which hears Judicial Reviews and applications for **habeas corpus**.

In some rare cases it may be possible to go to the House of Lords for a further appeal. This would normally be on a point of law rather than about a dispute on the facts of the case.

Anyone wanting to appeal needs permission, called 'leave to appeal'. This is only given when there is a genuine chance of a successful outcome or there are other strong reasons for allowing an appeal to proceed.

 Legal case: Tanfern Ltd v Cameron-MacDonald (2000)

In *Tanfern Ltd v Cameron-MacDonald (2000)* the Court of Appeal (Civil Division) explained that second appeals would become something of a rarity. The Government is keen to see this happen to reduce the considerable pressure currently on the civil court process. It was feared that the introduction of the **Human Rights Act 1998** would open a floodgate of claims and appeals. It was therefore felt that:

- only appeals with a real prospect of success should be allowed

- only one appeal for a civil case should be allowed, unless there were very exceptional circumstances

- the automatic right to appeal should be withdrawn and permission would be needed in almost all appeals to the Court of Appeal.

The predicted surge in demand for appeals generated by the **Human Rights Act 1998** has not happened to any great degree. The changes remain in force, however, and most people regard them as a 'qualified success'.

 Jargon buster

- **Appellate** means appeal.

- A person who feels that they are unlawfully held in custody can apply for **habeas corpus**. That person is then brought before the High Court Queen's Bench Division for a decision to be made on whether the detention is legal or not.

Fewer appeals

6 Problems of using the courts

Problems of cost, delay and complexity still deter many citizens with a legal issue from using the civil courts system.

Cost

Changes brought about by the **Access to Justice Act 1999** have made justice more achievable for some people, but they have possibly reduced it for others. Conditional fee arrangements/no win no fee have allowed many more people to access the civil court system, but problems remain for those clients with weaker cases and when solicitors attempt to increase their share of the 'winnings' from successfully completed cases. Some lawyers are increasingly seeing the civil case as a ready source of income and are quite happy to encourage litigation to 'solve' the dispute.

Delay

Significant delay was present in both County Court and High Court cases, although it is now getting a little better. Three years between the incident and the trial in the County Court and up to five years in the High Court were common. One result of this has been less effective trials since witnesses are hazy on events that happened so long ago, possibly under circumstances of panic and emergency.

The delay issue affects the financial and psychological status of some parties more than of others, of course. Businesses, local authorities or health trusts have no emotional involvement with a case. A sick or elderly claimant who is possibly using the civil system for the first time may feel differently. They may well suffer sleepless nights worrying about the cost and whether they were right to pursue the case, given the impact on their nerves and health.

Complexity

Legislation generated from UK and European sources may increase the complexity of civil cases. Legal representation then sometimes becomes essential, pushing up costs for both sides.

Out-of-court settlements

As a result of the problems of cost, delay and complexity, many ordinary claimants may accept woefully inadequate out-of-court settlements from the defendants. This is particularly true if the defendants are large companies or public bodies who have the resources to string the case out.

Lord Woolf

The problems of using the civil courts have been reduced to a certain extent by the Woolf Review proposals. Encouragement to use the many alternatives to the formal court process and a less adversarial approach have improved the process.

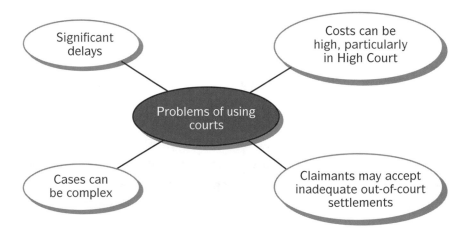

Problems of using the courts

Revision checklist

1 The County Courts are local courts designed to hear civil cases involving unpaid bills, personal injury cases and uncontested divorce cases.

2 Small claims track deals with cases involving sums of money less than £5000.

3 Fast track deals with sums of money between £5000 and £15 000.

4 Multi-track deals with cases involving sums of money greater than £15 000 or more complex cases.

5 The High Court deals with more important civil cases.

6 The High Court is split into three divisions which have corresponding Divisional Courts for appeals attached: Chancery Division, Queen's Bench Division and Family Division.

7 Jurisdiction of the courts refers to their power to hear a case. Overlapping powers make the civil court structure complex.

8 Appeals in the civil court system are normally to the next judge up: District Judges to Circuit Judges, Circuit Judges to High Court Judges.

9 Problems of using the civil court system include: cost, delay, complexity and out-of-court settlements.

10 Major reforms of the Civil Courts have occurred as a result of the Woolf Review 1996 and **Civil Procedure Act 1997**. Many of the reforms actually came into force in April 1999.

Quick revision questions

1 What are chief functions of the County Court?

2 What types of cases are heard in small, fast and multi-track?

3 What is the work of the three divisions of the High Court?

4 Where would a dispute involving £4500 of building work be heard?

5 Which court would deal with a personal injury case worth £250 000?

6 Where would an uncontested divorce case involving children be heard?

7 What does jurisdiction mean?

8 What is the main appeal principle in civil cases?

9 What are the main problems users encounter when using the courts?

10 Outline the key reforms brought about by the Woolf Review.

Exam question

1 *a* What are the main problems facing a claimant who wishes to take a case to the civil court? (15 marks)

   b How could an individual gain access to the civil court system more effectively? (15 marks)

Exam answer guide

1 *a* Possible problems that might arise could include:

   ✓ Costs such as legal fees, time off work to attend hearings and other expenses that could be involved in such an undertaking

   ✓ Costs of the other side if you lose a fast track or multi-track case

   ✓ Delay to the case might last for several weeks or months

   ✓ Complexity of the system that intimidates ordinary citizens

   ✓ Other side may be much more powerful, i.e. a business or local authority.

   Mention as many issues as you can think of, but focus on a limited number and develop some more in-depth points.

   b Possible solutions might include:

   ✓ Use of conditional fee arrangements/no win no fee

   ✓ Use of an advice agency or trade union for support

   ✓ Sorting out the problem before court hearing

   ✓ Use of a trade association, watchdog or media source for help

   ✓ Consider application for Community Legal Service funding

   ✓ *Pro bono* (free legal advice and representation).

   The answer would benefit from your view, so after you have considered the issue make sure you give an opinion on access to justice.

Unit 7

Alternatives to the courts

Why do I need to know about alternatives to courts?

Questions set on alternatives to courts are popular since this area is now seen as an important part of the Government's solution to pressure on the civil courts system. You need to understand the background to the reforms, the key alternatives suggested and how effective they are. The Legatt Report has reviewed the tribunal system and suggested improvements. Read the last unit on civil courts again to refresh your memory on the problems faced by users of the court system.

Alternative dispute resolution

1 Arbitration

The court system is under strain in a way unseen in its long history. People are resorting to the courts more often. The enormous rise in consumption of goods, more complex working patterns and greater confidence have increased the scope for disputes. Employees, consumers, patients and even students are resorting to the courts to get 'justice'. The result has been enormous pressure on the courts. The Woolf Reforms of the civil court system have attempted to reduce the burden on the courts and encourage a different approach to dispute solving, known as *alternative dispute resolution* (ADR).

Arbitration is one method to resolve disputes without court action. Both sides voluntarily agree to an independent third party making a decision on their case. The process in governed by the **Arbitration Act 1996**. The details of the case and the process are normally put into writing to keep everything clear. Arbitration is the most formal of the methods we will consider in this unit.

Arbitration style however can vary considerably, depending on the parties involved and their needs. It can range from very informal to a process which does not look unlike a formal court. The courts can enforce awards made by the arbitrator although, as in some formal civil cases, the claimant may in the end see little if any of the money promised.

Industrial arbitration

One of the best known organizations working in this area is the Arbitration and Conciliation Advisory Service (ACAS). ACAS is Government-funded. It often finds itself arbitrating between trade unions and employers in industrial disputes. ACAS has a record of being respected by both sides for its impartiality and effectiveness.

Consumer arbitration

Many organizations involved in the commercial world have introduced arbitration schemes to help relationships between consumers and businesses. The building industry has the Federation of Master Builders (FMB) and the travel industry has the Association of British Travel Agents (ABTA).

Commercial arbitration

The complexity of business contracts makes disputes likely. One way to limit the damage and expense caused by such disagreement is to have a safety valve built into any agreements. The two parties will seek arbitration if they cannot quickly solve a problem that arises between them. The *Scott v Avery (1855)* case signalled this new approach, so a clause in a contract pre-agreeing arbitration is called a Scott Avery Clause.

The arbitrator

Strengths of the arbitration system

- A knowledgeable arbitrator may have heard hundreds of similar cases.

- The facts of the arbitrated case are not public information, so companies and individuals who value privacy may prefer this style.

- Claimants and defendants can choose a time and place to suit them.

- Arbitration is normally quicker and cheaper than formal court procedures.

Weaknesses of the arbitration system

- Some claimants are disappointed that there is no public airing of the wrong done.

- There may be difficulties when the case covers technical legal points outside the capabilities of the participants.

- Awards can be challenged by either party when they believe serious irregularities have taken place.

- Individuals may still be much weaker if an organization is defending a case and seeks prior professional guidance.

Examination tip

A revision plan is essential. Organize your time properly before the examination.

2 Conciliation

Conciliation involves a neutral third party helping to solve a dispute. The conciliator raises relevant issues and actively suggests appropriate solutions. There are a number of official bodies which offer such support, including the Centre for Dispute Resolution. The service is quick and cheap, although the claimant and defendant are not bound by the process and can break off at any point if they choose. More formal and costlier processes may then of course have to be considered.

3 Mediation

Mediation involves an independent third party attempting to find some common ground between two parties in dispute. The mediator acts as a message carrier between the two. The process will only work if there really is some midway point that the two parties actively try to find acceptable. Relate is one well known organization offering a mediation service. Its services are available to any couple considering a legal divorce, or indeed any couple experiencing difficulties in their relationship.

An ombudsman is an independent third party who tries to solve disputes concerning poor service offered by public services. There are ombudsmen who deal with tax issues, with the National Health Service and with local government. The **Court and Legal Services Act 1990** introduced an ombudsman to deal with legal services and conveyancing (buying and selling houses).

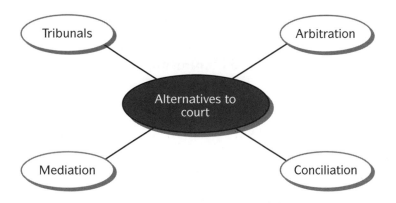

Alternatives to courts

The mediator

4 Role and composition of administrative tribunals

The Government sets up administrative tribunals. Their main function is to enforce citizen's rights to welfare and other social security entitlements. They have a wide jurisdiction that covers 75 different areas of life, with more than 2000 panels sitting to hear cases around the country. All decisions made by administrative tribunals can be judicially reviewed.

Some tribunals, such as the Social Security and National Insurance Tribunals, operate as a nationwide network, while others are proud of their independence.

Examples of administrative tribunals include:

- Social Security Appeals Tribunal
- Immigration Appeals Tribunal
- Mental Health Review Tribunal
- Rent Tribunals
- Employment Tribunals.

The Legatt Report reviewed the present system of tribunals in August 2001. It revealed that the 70 tribunals dealt with over a million cases per year. The Social Security Tribunal was the largest, hearing 270 000 appeals in one year. The Legatt Report recommended the following changes:

- better access to information and service
- a Customer Charter setting down standards to be reached

- improved tribunal procedures
- more use of information technology.

The development of the tribunal system is a little bit like the development of the courts system in general. The system has responded to changes over a period of time and now looks very chaotic and unstructured to the outsider. Most tribunals have similar features.

- The tribunal is set up as a panel of three individuals, one of whom is normally qualified or experienced in the area that the tribunal covers.
- The two lay members are expected to have some knowledge of the tribunal's work.
- The chairman is appointed by the Lord Chancellor's Department, and is therefore to a certain extent distanced from outside pressure.
- The process is often less formal than a court hearing.
- Apart from Employment Tribunals, precedent does not have to be followed.
- Decisions are not always supported by full explanations, which makes appeals difficult.

Domestic tribunals consider problems relating to their own professions, i.e. the British Medical Association represents doctors and the Bar Council represents barristers.

Strengths of the tribunal system

- Cases are normally dealt with more quickly and more cheaply than in the courts.
- Each tribunal has an expert, which in many ways is an advantage over a court which has to call in outside witnesses for specialist opinion.
- Procedure is more informal, which is of benefit to clients who are unfamiliar with putting their case in a public setting.
- The cases are heard in private, which can benefit business confidentiality and helps people with delicate issues to discuss.

Weaknesses of the tribunal system

- Power imbalance often exists between an individual and a large business or Government department.
- Giving no reasons for decisions makes meaningful appeals unlikely.
- Tax and social security legislation and procedures are so complex that clients without expert support are often at a disadvantage.
- Lack of funding for cases disadvantages individual claimants or defendants.

Web activity

For the background to the Legatt Review of the tribunal system see www.tribunals-review.org.uk.

Revision checklist

1 Arbitration allows an independent third party to make decisions on a dispute, if both parties agree.

2 It is possible to have industrial, consumer and commercial arbitration.

3 Strengths of arbitration include: knowledgeable arbitrator, privacy, cheaper and more convenient than courts.

4 Weaknesses of arbitration include: no publicity, technicalities may cause problems, awards can be challenged, and individuals weaker than large companies/public organizations.

5 Conciliation involves active approach to solving dispute.

6 Mediation involves trying to find common ground between two parties.

7 Ombudsmen investigate public bodies and their poor administration.

8 Administrative tribunals cover areas such as: social security, immigration, mental health, rent and employment.

9 Strengths of administrative tribunals include: speed, experts, informality and privacy.

10 Weaknesses of administrative tribunals include: power imbalance, no explanations for decisions, cases can be complex so individuals disadvantaged, and no legal funding for individuals.

Quick revision questions

1 What are the key elements to arbitration?

2 What types of arbitration are available?

3 Name three strengths of arbitration.

4 Name three weaknesses of arbitration.

5 What is the difference between conciliation and mediation?

6 What does an ombudsman do?

7 Name some key areas that administrative tribunals work in.

8 What report has recently reviewed the tribunal system?

9 What knowledge is expected of the members of a tribunal?

10 Name the key pros and cons of the tribunal system.

Exam question

1 *a* Why have ADR methods increased in recent years? (15 marks)

   b What are the main ways in which parties with civil disputes can resolve their differences? (15 marks)

Exam answer guide

1 *a* Include the following points

   ✓ Legal costs have increased

   ✓ Court delays and complexity

   ✓ Effectiveness of tribunals

   ✓ People with busy lives have no time for formal hearings

   ✓ Encouragement by the Government

   ✓ More information about alternatives available.

   Do not go into too much detail given the number of marks and what the question has asked. A brief outline is all that in needed.

   b Include the following points:

   ✓ Negotiation

   ✓ Mediation

   ✓ Conciliation

   ✓ Arbitration

   ✓ Tribunals

   ✓ Courts.

   Show some in-depth analysis by choosing one or two points to explore in more detail. Give your opinion. Do you think ADR is a better approach than using the courts?

1 Criminal law and *actus reus*

2 Criminal law and *mens rea*

3 The *actus reus* and *mens rea* of non-fatal offences

4 Strict liability

5 Sentences available to the criminal courts

6 Tort

7 Breach of duty of care

8 Capacity in crime and in tort

Crime and punishment

Unit 1 Criminal law and *actus reus*

Key points

1 Definition of criminal law
2 Aims of criminal law
3 Classification of criminal offences
4 Meaning of *actus reus*
5 *Actus reus* and causation

Why do I need to know about criminal law and actus reus?

Criminal law studies the most serious offences against members of society. This unit looks at the definition of crime and the physical elements of an act of crime. In legal terms the guilty act is known as the *actus reus*. It is one part of any crime that needs to be proved. The other part concerns the guilty mind, which you will study in the next unit. Criminal law can be complex, so make sure you grasp each element before you continue. Study of legal cases will be vital to your overall understanding. Questions on

Actus reus

actus reus and crime in this syllabus will focus on non-fatal offences against the person such as assault, battery, actual bodily harm and wounding and grievous bodily harm. Restrict yourself to these areas. It is important that you relate the law you learn carefully and thoughtfully to the case studies you will be presented with. This means that you must have a thorough understanding of the basic concepts of English criminal law.

1 Definition of criminal law

Criminal law deals with serious offences against the state or society. As these offences are so severe, the proof needed must be of a higher quality than that needed in other branches of the law. In the case where a defendant pleads not guilty, the prosecution must prove that the defendant is guilty 'beyond reasonable doubt'. If the prosecution can prove this, the jury will return a verdict of guilty and the judge then sentences the defendant. If the defendant pleads guilty, then the jury is not used. The judge listens to the case and passes a sentence.

Where a criminal law is broken, the state will consider prison. Prison is the harshest punishment used against an individual. Under recent guidance judges must consider all other options before imposing a prison sentence. Prison sentences are also known as *custodial* sentences.

Criminal law covers a wide range of offences, from traffic violations and shoplifting on the one hand to major crimes such as armed robbery and murder on the other. Minor criminal cases are heard in the Magistrates' Court. The more serious criminal cases are heard in the Crown Court. The Auld Report proposed that many more criminal offences should be switched from the Crown Court to the Magistrates' Court.

Perception of what is criminal

What is understood to be criminal conduct can vary from country to country and from one period in history to another. What is defined as 'criminal' will alter according to changes in society and changes in Government policy.

The attitude of society has gradually changed over time, and many things that were viewed as clearly criminal behaviour in Victorian times are now seen as acceptable, or at least non-criminal, by a large section of British society. Attitudes of society are often reflected in what is and is not covered in the Criminal Code.

Jargon buster

The **Criminal Code** covers types of behaviour which the legal system would classify as seriously anti-social. Note that some criminal law comes from Acts of Parliament and some from law made by judges which is known as common law.

Group activity

The area of law that deals with sexual behaviour has seen significant changes over the past 120 years.

1885   Homosexual acts between men in private are criminalized.

1967   Homosexual acts between men in private are decriminalized providing both men are over 21.

1994   Age of consent for gay men is reduced to eighteen.

2000   Age of consent for gay men is equalized with the rest of the adult population at sixteen years old.

There was never any legislation covering sexual behaviour between women.

1   Do you think the law should be used for personal and private behaviour?

2   Why did the law change over this period of time?

Group activity

Cannabis possession and use continue to be a topic of public debate. The use of this drug is still a criminal act, but the Government has reclassified it as a less serious substance, changing cannabis from a class B to a class C drug. Police will now usually caution offenders rather than take them to court. A typical sentence for possession of cannabis, before these recent changes, was a £25 fine.

1   What are the aims of criminal law in the area of illegal drugs?

2   Are there any alternatives to the use of criminal law to curb drug use?

3   Will and should such drug use ever become decriminalized?

2   Aims of criminal law

Criminal law has evolved through parliamentary legislation, but also through common law developed by the decisions of judges. Criminal law therefore reflects, or has at some time reflected, political and social values. Some law is so central to society's needs that there is little controversy. Murder, for example, is always seen as a serious criminal offence. At the other extreme, however, are moral positions on the drugs debate and euthanasia. The law seems less certain and more open to change in these controversial areas.

The aims of criminal law include:

- punishment by the state of those who commit serious offences against society

- the preservation of social order by drawing clear boundaries between what is and is not deemed acceptable social behaviour

- the protection of individuals, their families, their communities and their possessions

- the enforcing of moral values, particularly for those most at risk such as children and any others not in a position to defend their own interests

- providing a deterrent so that offenders do not repeat their crimes and others are persuaded to behave in a non-criminal way.

The law performs a difficult balancing act in protecting the rights of individual members of society whilst not damaging the legitimate rights of law-abiding individuals.

Research activity

Anti-terrorist legislation passed as the result of the attack on the World Trade Centre in September 2001 hopes to help law enforcement agencies protect society better and prevent attacks in the United Kingdom.

1 Find out the main elements to this legislation. Good places to look might be the Liberty website and the Home Office website to get some contrasting views.

2 Do these changes in the criminal law cause you any worries about freedom of thought, expression or human rights?

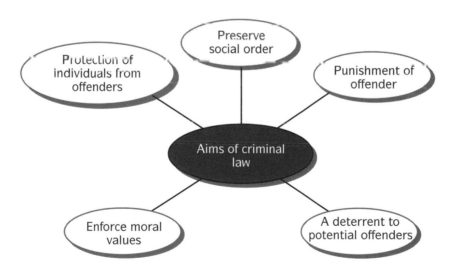

Aims of criminal law

Classification of criminal offences

Law classified by where case is heard

When you looked at the Magistrates' Courts in Module 2 Unit 1, you saw that offences were seen in different ways according to sentencing powers:

- **Summary offences** are heard by magistrates and are seen as the least serious crimes. They include disorderly conduct, minor shoplifting and non-payment of council tax.

- **Either way offences** can be heard in either the Magistrates' Court or the Crown Court depending on severity. Theft is a common example, since it can cover anything from an armed bank robbery to the shoplifting of a tin of beans.

- **Indictable offences** are seen as the most serious criminal offences and are only heard in the Crown Court. These offences include serious assaults and murder.

Law classified by source

Another important classification of criminal law is identifying which laws come to us from parliamentary legislation and which come from common law. There may be times when legislation is not as rapid as it needs to be, and judges decide that changes in social perspective need to be reflected in a change in the law.

Legal case: R v R (1991)

The case *R v R (1991)* illustrates a law changed not by Parliament but by judges. Up to then, women were assumed to have given their consent to sex by getting married, and rape within marriage therefore was not considered possible. Parliament had considered changing the law as early as 1976. Nothing was done, however, until the Court of Appeal and then the House of Lords decided the law had to be changed. Common law, made by the decisions of judges, took the lead, rather than parliamentary legislation made by our elected representatives.

Law classified by type of harm caused

- **Offences against the person** include assault and causing injury.

- **Offences against property** include theft, robbery and criminal damage.

- **Public order offences** are those such as affray, violent disorder and riot that would put a reasonable person in fear for their safety.

Revision card activity

Summarize the main ways criminal offences can be grouped.

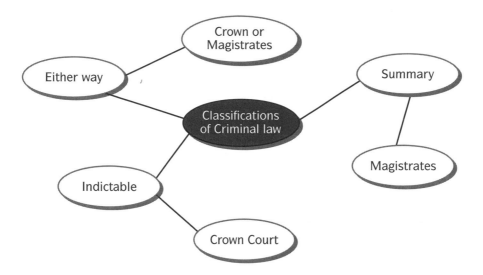

Classifications of criminal law

4 Meaning of *actus reus*

The term *actus reus* means 'the guilty act'. It forms part of a Latin phrase meaning: 'the act is only guilty if the mind is also guilty'. This section looks at the 'guilty act'.

Actus reus is an essential concept in criminal law. It must be present for there to be a criminal offence.

Voluntary act or omission

The defendant must have control over their actions or omissions. If they act out of reflex or because of some other force acting on them, it cannot be seen as voluntary, therefore they are not guilty. An example was given in the case of *Hill v Baxter (1958)* of a driver being stung by a swarm of bees. Clearly driving a car in these circumstances would be extremely difficult, and no one could be held liable for their actions.

For theft, the person must have 'appropriated the property of another', in other words taken the article without permission. A shoplifter who takes an article from a supermarket without paying for it has committed the *actus reus* element of the crime of theft.

For some crimes there must also be a consequence. The crime of murder clearly not only involves the unlawful act of shooting the victim but also requires the victim to die of those wounds. Murder has three distinct elements to form the *actus reus*:

1 An unlawful act (the conduct)

2 Committed under the Queen's peace (the circumstance)

3 Causes the death of another human being (the consequence).

The example of murder illustrates that *actus reus* is often actually a package of interdependent elements: conduct, circumstance and consequence. All must be present for the *actus reus* to be present.

Criminal damage also illustrates the idea that more than one element must be present for the *actus reus* to take shape. The **Criminal Damage Act 1971** requires the following:

1 Property to be damaged or destroyed (the conduct)

2 No lawful excuse (the circumstance)

3 The property to be actually destroyed (the consequence).

Omissions and actus reus

The *actus reus* is generally a voluntary act, but there are circumstances where an omission will also be considered to be *actus reus*. One such situation is when a duty of care is created. This can be illustrated by the following legal case-study.

Legal case: R v Gibbons and Proctor (1918)

The case of *R v Gibbons and Proctor (1918)* illustrated the duty of care that existed by the presence of a parent/child relationship. Gibbons, the girl's father, allowed his daughter to starve to death. He and the woman he was living with were found guilty of murder. The father's duty of care made his omission the *actus reus* of the crime.

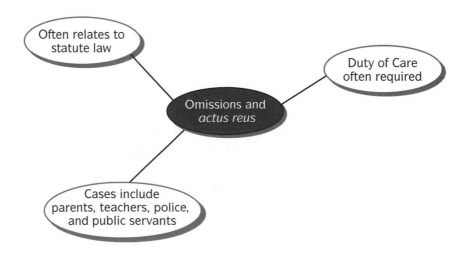

Omissions and actus reus

Sometimes a duty of care exists via legislation, as in reporting road accidents. This is often referred to as a *statutory duty*. Other duties of care may exist between parents and children, teachers and pupils, doctors and patients and even between motorists and other motorists. An omission may form part of a criminal case, the *actus reus*.

Legal case: R v Pittwood (1902)

In *R v Pittwood (1902)* a gatekeeper on a railway level crossing failed to close the gate after allowing a car through. Some time later a passing train killed the owner of a second vehicle. The gatekeeper was found guilty of **manslaughter**. The court stated that a person might incur criminal liability from not carrying out part of a contract. His omission to close the gate became the *actus reus* of the crime.

People are not generally required to act the hero and save others from burning buildings. If, however, they have themselves created the dangerous circumstance, then they have a duty towards possible victims. *R v Miller (1983)* illustrates this situation.

Legal case: R v Miller (1983)

In *R v Miller (1983)* a squatter smoking a cigarette accidentally set fire to his mattress. He then moved into the next room without putting the fire out or alerting anyone else. He was found guilty of arson under the **Criminal Damage Act 1971**. His omission became the *actus reus* of the crime.

Jargon buster

Manslaughter occurs when an unlawful act results in a death that was not intended or the person who committed the offence was not responsible for their actions.

Group activity

A strong and fit swimmer walking past a lake sees a toddler in the water struggling for life. The swimmer, who is late for an appointment, keeps on walking and gives no assistance to the helpless child. The youngster drowns. The swimmer is not criminally liable. He has done nothing wrong as far as the law is concerned.

1 What are your views on the case?

2 Can you think of any reasons why the law does not force a duty of care on all of us to help our fellow citizens?

R v Miller (1983)

5 *Actus reus* and causation

Causation in fact

If a criminal case is to be proved, then it must be shown that the conduct of the defendant caused the consequence. There must be a clear and unbroken link between conduct and consequence. The 'but for' rule is used to help out in these cases, as shown with *R v Pagett (1983)*.

Legal case: R v Pagett (1983)

R v Pagett (1983) illustrated conduct and consequence working together. Pagett used his girlfriend as a shield when firing a gun at the police. The police returned fire and killed the girlfriend. Pagett was found guilty of her unlawful death, even though it was police bullets that killed her. It was stated that holding the girl in front of him and firing at the police were both unlawful and dangerous acts that contributed to the *actus reus*. His contribution was not the main contribution to her death, but she would not have been put into the position 'but for' him. He was found guilty of manslaughter.

There are times, however, when even if the defendant intended the consequence, his or her actions may fail to produce the consequence.

Legal case: R v White (1910)

In the case of *R v White (1910)* a son attempted to poison his mother. The mother died of a heart attack unconnected to the potassium cyanide put into her drink. The son was not convicted of murder. It was not the defendant's act that caused the consequence, despite his ambition to see her dead. He was, however, found guilty of attempted murder. The 'but for' rule would not apply because the poor woman would have died anyway.

Causation in law

To prove legal cause, the defendant must contribute to the consequences. The contribution must be more than minimal, but it does not have to be substantial. It may also be the case that others had a part to play, but the defendant may still be held liable. *R v Smith (1959)* illustrates legal causation even in the most bizarre circumstances.

Legal case: R v Smith (1959)

A British soldier in Germany named Smith stabbed another soldier. The injured victim was dropped twice on the journey to hospital and then received inadequate medical care. The court ruled that despite the appalling treatment the victim had received at the hands of the medical unit, Smith was still guilty of the death. The events did not break the chain of causation.

In the above case, Smith began the chain of events that led to the death of the victim. The intervening acts did not break this chain of events, according to the court. In fact, it may be said that courts are fairly reluctant to allow a defendant 'off' due to intervening acts breaking the chain of causation. *R v Blaue (1975)* and *R v Cheshire (1991)* are two important cases that reflect this tendency of the courts.

Legal case: R v Blaue (1975)

In *R v Blaue (1975)* an 18-year-old girl was attacked and stabbed in the lung. She was taken to hospital but refused a blood transfusion because of her religious beliefs. The attacker, Blaue, was convicted of manslaughter on the grounds of diminished responsibility. He appealed against this conviction on the grounds that it was the girl's own act that caused her death. The appeal was dismissed and the judge stated that offenders **'must take their victim as they find them'**. The intervening act did not break the chain of causation.

Legal case: R v Cheshire (1991)

The attacker in *R v Cheshire (1991)* shot the victim in the leg and stomach, wounding him seriously. The victim was taken to hospital where he developed complications from his medical treatment and died eight weeks later. The Court of Appeal stated that only 'in the most extraordinary and unusual case' would medical treatment be regarded as the cause of the victim's death. The intervening act did not break the chain of causation.

A number of other cases involving medical intervention illustrate the courts' general views. Medical advances have posed problems for the courts. It is now possible to keep people 'alive' for long periods of time, although it might be fair to say that it is only their body rather than their mind that is still functioning. A case that clarified this difficult area of law came in 1981.

Legal case: R v Malcherek (1981)

In *R v Malcherek (1981)* a husband stabbed his wife repeatedly and she was put on a life-support machine. The medical team switched off the life-support machine when it was decided that recovery of the victim was not going to happen. Malcherek put forward the defence that it was the action of turning off the machine that caused death. The Court of Appeal decided that the intervening act did not break the chain of causation. Malcherek was responsible for the death, and not the doctors. The Court of Appeal went further to say that they thought the argument that Malcherek had not caused death was 'bizarre'.

Intervening acts and a break in the chain

We have looked at several cases where the chain of events was not broken despite people intervening. The chain of causation can be broken by the following circumstances:

- Actions of a third party (not the victim or the defendant)
- The victim's own contribution to events
- A natural event which could not have been foreseen.

Jargon buster

'**Taking your victim as you find them**' is also known as the *thin skull rule*. The criminal cannot blame the victim for having some sort of weakness that results in a more serious injury than intended.

Legal case **R v Jordan (1956)**

The victim of a stabbing was given a medication called terramycin in such large doses and in such an inappropriate way that it has flooded his lungs and killed him. In fact, by the time of death, the stab wounds had virtually healed. The defence was able to argue successfully that the medical treatment was so awful that their client should be found not guilty of the victim's death.

Examination tip

Thorough knowledge and good evaluation skills when you express your views will give the highest marks.

Intervening acts

Revision checklist

1 Criminal law deals with offences against society. These offences range from the most minor to the most serious.

2 Prison is a possible punishment, so the case must 'be proved beyond reasonable doubt'.

3 Aims of criminal law include: punishing offenders, preserving order, protection of individuals, enforcing moral views, and deterrence.

4 Criminal law can be classified by where it is heard, who makes it and who it affects.

5 *Actus reus* means 'the guilty act'. It can also be a failure to act. This is known as an omission but it only applies where there is a duty of care.

6 *Actus reus* usually consists of various elements including: conduct, circumstance and consequence.

7 Causation means the conduct of the defendant and the consequences of his or her actions can be linked together.

8 Causation in fact uses the 'but for' rule.

9 Causation in law looks at the contribution the defendant's conduct made to the consequence, even if there have been intervening acts by others.

10 The defence often uses the impact of intervening acts. Courts have seldom accepted this as breaking the chain of events.

Quick revision questions

1 Define criminal law.

2 What are the key aims of criminal law?

3 Name the three main classes of offence.

4 Why was *R v R (1991)* an important case?

5 Define *actus reus*.

6 Why was *R v Gibbons and Proctor (1918)* important as far as omissions were concerned?

7 Name two examples where statutory law has placed a duty of care on the defendant.

8 How is the 'but for' rule used with *actus reus*?

9 How did *R v Malcherek (1981)* explore the issue of causation?

10 Name three circumstances that break the rules of causation.

Exam question

1 a Describe the meaning of a crime. (10 marks)

   b What problems do the courts face when trying to prove *actus reus*? (20 marks)

Exam answer guide

1 a Criminal acts are the most serious offences against society and the community. Some vary from community to community and from one time in history to another. Others, such as murder, are nearly always regarded as the most serious offences. Crime is dealt with by a range of punishments, from small fines up to long periods of imprisonment. Criminal law aims to punish, deter and rehabilitate.

   b Possible points include:

✓ Some crimes include: conduct, circumstance and consequence

✓ Duty of care complications

✓ Can be problems with *actus reus* and causation

✓ Intervening acts

✓ Defence teams

✓ Evidence.

Criminal cases involve severe punishments and a criminal record. It is important that the case is conducted fairly and thoroughly, with protection for the defendant as well as consideration for the victim.

Unit 2 Criminal law and *mens rea*

Why do I need to know about **mens rea?**

For most crimes it is not enough to prove that the person committed the crime; it is necessary to show a criminal state of mind as well. *Mens rea* means 'guilty mind'. There is a strong link between the last unit on *actus reus* (the guilty act) and this one on *mens rea*. Both are required before a person is found guilty of a criminal offence. There are

Coincidence of actus reus *and* mens rea

some fascinating cases used in the exploration of these ideas. Make sure you know them. Put them onto revision cards and learn them. Think about the people involved and the fairness of the situations they find themselves in. You can even apply these ideas in day-to-day events in your own life. Get familiar with the concepts.

1 Mens rea

The *mens rea* of an offence is the guilty mind associated with that offence. It concerns the mental elements involved in a crime. Both the guilty act and the guilty mind must be present if a person is to be convicted of a criminal offence. *Actus reus* and *mens rea* are required.

The shop where goods have been stolen might have the incident on CCTV. They may possess the videotape and take it to court as proof of the defendant's guilt. The court, however, must be satisfied that the person had it in their mind to take the goods without paying for them. Possible defences might include:

- a medical condition or medication which lowers the ability to concentrate
- fatigue, which may increase absent-mindedness
- stress caused by family or work problems
- old age
- premenstrual syndrome.

The court may take these factors into consideration when deciding whether a person deliberately attempted to steal from the shop. These are known as *extenuating circumstances*: situations that may temporarily affect a person's judgement.

Legal case: R v Madely (1990)

Richard Madely, presenter of the popular TV shows *This Morning* and *Richard and Judy*, found himself in court charged with shoplifting from a major supermarket. The store had witnesses and other evidence to 'prove' the guilty act took place. The court, however, accepted the star's defence that overwork and stress had led him to forget to pay for the goods. The *actus reus* was proved but not the *mens rea*.

Each criminal offence has its own *mens rea*. The minimum level of *mens rea* must be proved if the prosecution is to win its case.

Group activity: R v Hart (2002)

The driver of a Land Rover skidded off the motorway at Selby and ended up on railway tracks, causing a major train crash. Ten people were killed, and Mr Hart was charged with dangerous driving. He had been on the Internet/phone for most of the night but maintained that he was normally competent to drive under such conditions. He was found guilty and jailed for five years. The maximum for dangerous driving would have been ten years.

1 Should Mr Hart have been jailed?

2 Did *mens rea* exist in this case?

---

2 Specific intent, direct intent and oblique intent

Specific intent is also known as *intent*. It is the highest level of *mens rea*. In other words, the defendant must have clearly had this outcome in mind and not committed the offence by accident or carelessness. It must have been their unmistakable goal. It must be proved by the prosecution in cases of murder and grievous bodily harm with intent.

Put legally, specific intent involves proving whether a person committed an act with purpose of the consequence or had the knowledge that the consequence was virtually certain to occur. The concept is seen more fully in *R v Mohan (1976)* and *Hyam v DPP (1974)*.

Legal case: R v Mohan (1976)

The case involved a serious driving charge which led to a wounding. The Court of Appeal heard the case and stated that 'intent' was 'a decision to bring about an offence'. It did not matter that the defendant failed or succeeded in their attempt, only that the defendant was trying to commit the illegal act. In addition, the chance of a successful criminal outcome was irrelevant. The key issue to prove for intention was the *decision* to try to commit the criminal act. This case clearly relates closely to *Hyam v DPP* (1974) in terms of intention. In both cases, intent is difficult to prove.

Legal case: Hyam v DPP (1974)

Pearl Hyam was jealous of Mrs Booth. She thought that the woman was about to get married to her former boyfriend. To scare her off, she set fire to her rival's house. Mrs Booth escaped but two of her children were killed. Pearl Hyam was charged with manslaughter, but was she guilty of murder? Did she intend to kill the two children? If she were only guilty of manslaughter, what would it have taken to prove the *mens rea* for murder?

Oblique intent

When a person desires the result of their actions, it is known as *direct intent*. Therefore if a person traces the movements of their victim, plans when to attack them and carries out an attack that results in the consequences they had planned, this would be regarded as direct intent. Everything has gone to plan, and the attacker is happy with the result.

If the person carries out the attack and produces another consequence that they did not intend but knew was likely to occur, this is known as *oblique intent*. Therefore, if the attacker plans to murder someone by exploding a bomb under the victim's car and as a side result destroys nearby houses, then the oblique intent is the demolition of the houses. This was very likely to happen if an explosive device was detonated in a street full of houses.

There are a number of interlinked cases where this concept has been explored and developed. The courts were clearly not entirely happy with the earlier cases and tried to improve the clarity of the argument each time.

Legal cases: R v Maloney (1985), R v Hancock and Shankland (1986), R v Nedrick (1986) *and* R v Woolin (1998)

R v Maloney (1985): The defendant shot and killed his stepfather in a 'game' that went tragically wrong. Both were drunk and trying to decide who was fastest on the draw. It was decided by the court that oblique intent would, in this case, mean manslaughter.

R v Hancock and Shankland (1986): Two defendants, attempting to intimidate a fellow worker during a strike, threw a concrete block from a bridge onto the victim's passing car. The victim was killed. The court focused on the probability of the consequence when using it as evidence to decide intent. Manslaughter was proved.

R v Nedrick (1986): The defendant poured petrol through the letterbox of a house to frighten the woman living there. The result was the death of a child. From this particular case two questions emerged which it was hoped would clarify the issue.

1 Was the result a virtual certainty of the action?

2 Did the defendant realize that the result would be a virtual certainty of his action?

Unless the jury was happy that the answer to both questions was 'yes', they could not assume the defendant's intention.

R v Woolin (1998): the defendant threw his three-month-old baby at his pram. The baby missed the pram and crashed into the wall. He died of his injuries. The courts were not happy with the two questions used in the Nedrick case, but still wanted the jury to 'find' intention only if they thought the result was a virtual certainty from the actions of the defendant and he knew this to be the case.

Examination tip

The definitions of intent that are being used by the courts are very complex. Don't be put off by these cases. They are difficult for most students, not to mention lawyers, judges and juries. Learn the names and facts of the cases carefully. Good quality references to authorities impress examiners.

3   Subjective recklessness

Subjective recklessness means the taking of an unjustifiable risk. The defendant recognizes that there is a risk, but continues with his or her actions. Subjective recklessness is a lower level of *mens rea* than specific intention. The accused is judged from what they believed to be the case. Did the defendant realize that what they were doing involved some risk of harm to someone else? It is linked to crimes such as common assault, actual bodily harm and malicious wounding, or indeed most crimes that include recklessness as the *mens rea*.

R v Cunningham (1957) highlighted the issues around subjective recklessness.

 ## Legal case: R v Cunningham (1957)

In *R v Cunningham (1957)* the defendant tore a gas meter from the wall of a cellar in order to steal the money contained inside it. The gas leaked from the exposed pipes through the cellar wall and drifted up through the next house where it injured a woman. The defendant did nothing to stop the gas escape. The word 'maliciously' was used in the case and became defined as either:

● intending the harm that resulted, or

● being reckless and realizing there was a possibility that the harm would result.

The second point came to be known as *subjective recklessness*.

There was no assumption in the above case that Cunningham was trying to injure the woman next door. The court did, however, assume that he should have realized that his actions may have led to an injury, but continued with his actions anyway. The defendant behaved recklessly in taking an unjustified risk and he, the subject, should have known better. The case is so often quoted that subjective recklessness is often called *Cunningham recklessness*.

Recklessness

4 Objective recklessness

Objective recklessness is used where the defendant does not realize that there is a risk of certain undesirable consequences, but an ordinary person would have realized the risk. As a result this is seen as a lower level of *mens rea* than subjective recklessness, where the person was assumed to understand the risks involved.

This test of what should have been realized employs the idea of what an ordinary, prudent person would have realized. *MPC v Caldwell (1982)* is the classic illustration of this issue.

Legal case: MPC v Caldwell (1982)

Caldwell was employed by a hotel and held a grievance against the owner. During a drunken binge he set fire to the hotel. He was charged with arson under the **Criminal Damage Act 1971**, but also with reckless behaviour leading to the endangering of life. The key point thrown up by the case was not whether Caldwell realized that this was reckless behaviour, but whether an 'ordinary prudent person' would have realized this. The **objective test** was being employed.

The Caldwell case attempted to define the word *recklessness*. A result of the case was a sharper definition of the term *reckless* which now had to be considered:

● The defendant has given no thought to the consequences of their actions, or

● The defendant realizes the risk from their actions but continues all the same.

The case is so often used that objective recklessness is often known as *Caldwell recklessness*.

Jargon buster

Subjective tests consider what the *defendant* would believe to be the case. **Objective tests** consider what *an ordinary person* would believe to be the case.

Group activity

Highlight the differences between subjective and objective recklessness using the subjective and objective test. Use three of your own examples to illustrate them. What are the problems of using such tests?

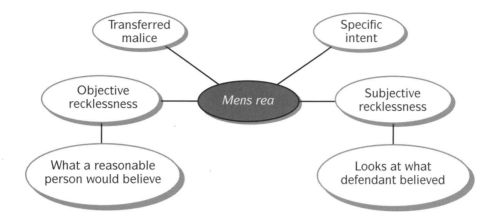

Mens rea

5 Transferred malice

If a person commits an unlawful act against one person which actually injures another, can they get away with the unplanned injury? The courts think not, and have developed a term called *transferred malice*. For example, if person A intends to run down pedestrian B in his car but accidentally crashes into pedestrian C, person A will be held responsible for C's injuries. Liability cannot be denied. The *mens rea* is transferred.

Legal case: R v Latimer (1886)

R v Latimer (1886) illustrated the concept of transferred malice. When Latimer attempted to strike his intended victim, he missed and hit a woman nearby. She was seriously injured. He was held liable for her injury. The *mens rea* was transferred from his intended victim to his actual victim.

The offences involved in transferred malice must be of the same nature. Therefore Latimer could be charged with injuring the woman in the manner in which he had intended to injury his original victim. If they are different, however, a case could still be made using recklessness as the *mens rea* of the offence. So if Latimer had broken a nearby window as he struck his victim, he might be said to have been behaving recklessly.

6 Coincidence of *actus reus* and *mens rea*

The last unit looked at *actus reus*, the guilty act and this unit at *mens rea*, the guilty mind. When they come together and both can be proved, there is a criminal offence. The two must come together or be close to one another in time.

Legal case: R v Taaffe (1983)

Mr Taaffe was intercepted by customs and his car was searched. Small packages of cannabis were found. When questioned, Mr Taaffe revealed that he thought it was money being illegally imported into the UK against currency regulations. This was not at the time a crime. He was convicted of illegally importing cannabis. The Court of Appeal and the House of Lords both confirmed that without the *mens rea* for importing cannabis, no offence had been committed. The *actus reus* was present since the drugs had been imported, but not the *mens rea*.

Fagan v Metropolitan Police Commissioner (1968) explores some of the issues of coincidence of *actus reus* and *mens rea*.

Legal case: Fagan v Metropolitan Police Commissioner (1968)

Police Constable David Morris observed Vincent Fagan driving irregularly. The police officer directed Fagan towards the kerb and stood a couple of metres in front of the car. Fagan parked the car tyre on the police officer's foot. The police officer asked Fagan to move the car but Fagan told the police officer he would have to wait. Fagan was again asked to move and eventually did. Fagan stated he moved onto the policeman's foot accidentally, that he had no intention and did not behave recklessly. If this were so, there would be no *mens rea*. Fagan continued to keep his car tyre on the policeman's foot, however. If an act continues, then the *mens rea* can come into play at a later time. Refusing to move when told to was seen as the *mens rea*.

The Fagan case involves what is known as the Continuing Act Theory. The *mens rea* was not present at the beginning of the *actus reus*, but appeared during it. The eventual coincidence of *actus reus* and *mens rea* therefore produced a criminal offence.

Revision checklist

1   The *mens rea* is the mental element to a crime. It is the guilty mind associated with the guilty act.

2   Specific intent is also known as intent. This is very difficult to prove. It is the highest level of *mens rea*. It is the guiltiest mind.

3   Direct intent relates to the aim of the offender.

4   If the offender carries out a guilty act but the result is not what they intended, this is called the *oblique intent*.

5   Subjective recklessness involves the taking of an unjustifiable risk. The defendant recognizes that there is a risk, but continues with their actions. It is also known as Cunningham Recklessness.

6   Objective recklessness occurs where the defendant does not realize that there is a risk of certain undesirable consequences but an ordinary person would have realized the risk. This is also known as Caldwell recklessness.

7   Transferred malice occurs when the defendant injures someone by 'mistake' when trying to injure someone else. They still have the *mens rea*. It is transferred to the 'innocent victim'.

8   *Actus reus* and *mens rea* must occur at the same time or close to each other for there to be a criminal offence.

9   *R v Taaffe (1983)* shows that when the *mens rea* was not present, the defendant was innocent.

10   *Fagan v Metropolitan Police Commissioner (1968)* showed a case of *mens rea* occurring during the *actus reus*.

Quick revision questions

1   Describe *mens rea*.

2   What is the relationship between *mens rea* and *actus reus*?

3   What are specific intent, direct intent and oblique intent?

4   What is subjective recklessness?

5   How does the case of *R v Cunningham (1957)* illustrate subjective recklessness?

6   What is objective recklessness?

7   How does the case of *MPC v Caldwell (1982)* illustrate objective recklessness?

8   What is transferred malice?

9   What does the case *R v Taaffe (1983)* show about the coincidence of *mens rea* and *actus reus*?

10   What does the case of *Fagan v Metropolitan Police Commissioner (1968)* show about the coincidence of *mens rea* and *actus reus*?

Exam question

1 a What is the difference between specific intent and recklessness? (15 marks)

  b Using cases, distinguish between the concepts of subjective recklessness and objective recklessness. (15 marks)

Exam answer guide

1 a Specific intent is the highest level of *mens rea*. It is associated with very serious crime, including murder and grievous bodily harm. The penalties for such crimes are very harsh, so the prosecution must prove beyond a reasonable doubt that the offender had a clear and specific intention to commit the crime. Recklessness involves a much lower degree of *mens rea*. It concerns behaviour where the offender knew there was a risk and yet continued with the action or had the intent to commit such an act. It is often associated with crimes such as assault and actual bodily harm.

  b Subjective recklessness is about what the defendant believed in terms of risky behaviour. Objective recklessness is about what a reasonable person would believe to be reckless behaviour. The key cases associated with these concepts are *R v Cunningham (1957)* (subjective) and *MPC v Caldwell (1982)* (objective).

Unit

The *actus reus* and *mens rea* of non-fatal offences

Why do I need to know about the actus reus *and* mens rea *of non-fatal offences?*

The ideas covered in the previous two units can now be used to explore non-fatal offences such as assault and grievous bodily harm. The vast majority of legislation is covered in a single piece of law called the **Offences Against the Person Act 1861**. It uses some important words which you should take care to use properly, such as *maliciously*, *grievously* and *intentionally*. Learn what the words mean and also remember

Non-fatal offences

the correct spellings of these words. Examiners' reports often mention students spelling these frequently used legal words incorrectly.

1 Common assault

As you saw earlier, *actus reus* means 'guilty act' and *mens rea* means 'guilty mind'.

The *actus reus* of common assault is:

● putting a person in fear of immediate unlawful violence, i.e. assault, or

● the application of unlawful force to a person, i.e. battery

The *mens rea* of common assault is:

● the intention or recklessness to put a person in fear of immediate unlawful force, or

● the intention or recklessness to apply unlawful force to a person.

Although assault and battery used to be two separate offences, Section 40 of the **Criminal Justice Act 1988** refers to them collectively as common assault. In the more serious offences we will look at later in this unit, the *actus reus* and *mens rea* of common assault are used as a foundation for the consideration of *actus reus* and *mens rea*. To understand the elements of common assault we can look at them separately.

Assault

Assault occurs when a person is put in fear of immediate and unlawful violence. There does not have to be any contact for this offence to take place. If someone is shaking his or her fist at you from across the road and you fear immediate and unlawful violence is going to occur, then you have been assaulted. Assault could occur via a threatening telephone call, e-mail or text message, provided the victim feared immediate unlawful violence against them.

The offence is defined in Section 39 of the **Criminal Justice Act 1988** as a summary offence which carries a maximum sentence of six months in prison or a fine.

 Legal case: R v Ireland (1997)

Malicious telephone calls made by Ireland amounted to assault. This was an important case since it underlined the fact that words or even silence can put the victim in fear of immediate violence.

The offender could, however, escape prosecution for assault by using words that made their real intention clear. For example: a dispute about parking which leads an older man to raise his fists to a younger man with the words: 'If I were your age, you'd be on your back with a thick lip' would hopefully reassure the victim that force was not going to be used, therefore there is no assault.

Legal case: Turberville v Savage (1669)

'If it were not **assize** time I would not take such language'. The aggressor had his hand on his sword when these words were spoken over 300 years ago. The victim was presumably reassured that he was not about to be run through with the blade. Immediate violence was not probable at this stage (but maybe later).

This case underlines the fact that the threat of unlawful force must be immediate. Once the assizes were over, possibly the sword would be drawn and used.

The offence is clearly context-based and depends on who the 'aggressor' is and who the 'victim' is. Sizes of the individuals, gender, age, disability, sexuality, race and culture may all play a part in what is considered and not considered assault.

Racially aggravated assault is seen as a more serious crime and is punishable by up to two years in prison. This change in the law came about through the **Crime and Disorder Act 1998**.

Assault

Battery

Battery occurs when physical contact takes place between the offender and the victim, no matter how small that contact. It is the application of unlawful force, whether intentionally or recklessly, on another person.

Battery does not have to be direct. In *Fagan v Metropolitan Police Commissioner (1968)* a car was used in the battery. *DPP v K (a minor) (1990)* shows an even more distant link between the defendant and the victim.

DPP v K (a minor) (1990)

A young chemistry student filled a hot-air dryer with acid when visiting the toilet. The next person who used the dryer was sprayed with acid. Although the force was indirect, K was held liable and charged with battery. The force does not have to be direct for a charge of battery.

Jargon buster

- The **Assizes** were courts that travelled from one town to another. They took the King's justice around the country. Judges still travel to the various Crown Courts and High Courts today.

- **Aggravated** means the use of greater force or worse behaviour than normal to make the situation more serious, i.e. aggravated burglary may involve vandalism as well as theft.

Did you know?

The layman's use of the term *assault* is technically wrong, but is so widespread that even some judges seem to accept it. The judge in *Fagan v Metropolitan Police Commissioner (1968)* stated during the trial that:

'assault is an independent crime but for practical purposes today is generally synonymous with the term "battery"'.

The layperson sees assault as making physical contact with someone.

Examination tips

- For recklessness in assault consider quoting *R v Cunningham (1957)*. This is known as subjective recklessness.

- Strong candidates weigh up the arguments for and against and then give their considered opinion.

2 Assault causing actual bodily harm

The *actus reus* of assault causing actual bodily harm is:

● Common assault

plus

● Actual bodily harm took place.

The *mens rea* of assault causing actual bodily harm is:

● Intention to cause fear of immediate unlawful force in a person *or* recklessness in not considering that a person might be put in fear of immediate unlawful force

An assault which causes an injury to the victim is generally seen as a more serious offence. The attack is defined under Section 47 of the **Offences Against the Person Act 1861**, where it is prohibited to carry out 'any assault occasioning bodily harm'. The word *occasion* means 'causing'.

This crime must have an outcome, i.e. actual bodily harm. 'Actual bodily harm' is taken to mean something more than trivial but less than really serious. It may include bruises and minor abrasions. The victim must have been made uncomfortable by the assault. The harm may include psychiatric harm. If this is the case, it must be recognized as a medical condition. It cannot include fear or anxiety, for example.

The two following legal cases, *R v Spratt (1991)* and *R v Savage (1991)* will give you an idea of what is covered by this offence.

Legal case: R v Spratt (1991)

A young girl was hit twice by a boy firing an airgun from his bedroom window. He admitted the action to the police, but in his defence said that he was only trying to see how far the pellets would travel. He was found guilty of assault occasioning actual bodily harm.

Legal case: R v Savage (1991)

An argument in a pub resulted in the defendant throwing beer over the victim. As she was doing this, the glass slipped from her hand and cut the victim's wrist. The court could not prove whether the injury caused by the glass was intentional. The court eventually decided that throwing beer over the victim was sufficient *mens rea* and therefore the accused was guilty under Section 47 of the **Offences Against the Person Act**.

Clearly the range of cases could be great, and the offence is therefore triable either way in the Magistrates' or Crown Court and carries a maximum prison sentence of five years.

Quick question

Using a spider diagram, demonstrate the differences between assault and battery and assault occasioning actual bodily harm. Include the *actus reus* and *mens rea* for each.

3 Malicious wounding/inflicting grievous bodily harm

The *actus reus* of malicious wounding/inflicting grievous bodily harm is:

● Unlawful wounding *or* unlawful infliction of grievous bodily harm.

The *mens rea* of malicious wounding/inflicting grievous bodily harm is:

● Intention to inflict harm *or* realizing there was a risk of harm but carrying on all the same, i.e. subjective recklessness.

Malicious wounding/inflicting grievous bodily harm is an offence under the **Offences Against the Person Act 1861**. Section 20 of the act states:

'Whoever unlawfully and maliciously wounds or inflicts grievous bodily harm (either with or without a weapon) shall be guilty of an offence'.

Note that malicious wounding or grievous bodily harm make the offence. The offence itself is called *malicious wounding*. The offence is triable either way and carries a maximum sentence of five years.

Each word in this section has a very specific meaning. It is a good idea to take each one separately and try to understand its meaning before putting the whole lot together.

Malicious

The word malicious was defined in *R v Cunningham (1957)*. It means that the defendant either:

● intended the harm to happen as a result of his or her actions, *or*

● knew there was a risk of harm but continued to carry out the actions anyway.

The term *malicious* refers to the state of mind of the defendant, not the injury. Malicious wounding does not require the defendant to realize that a serious injury would result. Even if the defendant intended or foresaw a minor injury and the injury caused was serious, the defendant still has the *mens rea* required for the more serious offence.

Wounding

Wounding requires a break in the whole skin of the person attacked. Even the most minor cut could then be classified as a wound. If someone was attacked with a baseball bat and suffered major internal injuries that did not result in external bleeding, this would not be a wound. It might be classified as a serious injury, particularly if the person had hospital treatment, but legally it would be actual bodily harm, not wounding. *JJC (a minor) v Eisenhower (1983)* illustrates this.

Legal case: JJC (a minor) v Eisenhower (1983)

The victim was hit in the eye by a pellet fired from an airgun. The pellet ruptured vessels in the eye but did not cause external bleeding. The court's view, considering the definition of a wound in Section 20 of the the **Offences Against the Person Act**, was that this was not a wound.

Grievous bodily harm

Grievous bodily harm means a serious injury. It consists of either:

- unlawful wounding (see above), *or*

- infliction of serious bodily harm.

Either of the above is enough for the *actus reus* for this offence, although of course both may be present in a serious attack.

Grievous bodily harm is an offence under Section 20 of the **Offences Against the Person Act 1861**. It carries a penalty of up to five years in prison.

Quick question

What wound would cause grievous bodily harm, i.e. a serious injury?

4 Wounding or causing grievous bodily harm with intent

The *actus reus* of wounding or causing grievous bodily harm with intent is:

- unlawful wounding, *or*

- unlawful infliction of grievous bodily harm.

This is the same as for wounding or causing grievous bodily harm.

The *mens rea* for wounding or causing grievous bodily harm with intent is:

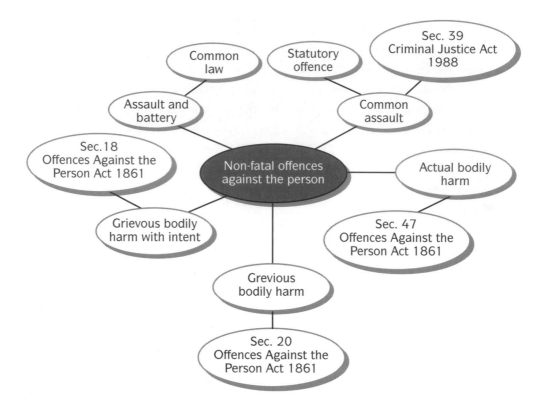

Non-fatal offences against the person

- intention to inflict grievous bodily harm, *or*

- intention to resist arrest and causing harm in the process intentionally or recklessly.

This offence is dealt with under Section 18 of the **Offences Against the Person Act 1861**. It is seen as the most serious non-fatal offence against a person. It is the intention and therefore the *mens rea* of the defendant that makes this offence different from the Section 20 offence. The distinction therefore is:

- Section 20: the intention is to cause some harm and the offence carries five years maximum prison sentence.

- Section 18: the intention is to cause grievous bodily harm and the offence carries life imprisonment as the maximum sentence.

This offence also includes the situation where the defendant has used force to resist arrest or aids another person to resist arrest. This is seen by the law as a very serious matter and carries the heavier prison sentence.

Offences against the Persons Act 1861

5 | Law Commission proposals for reform

If you have been following this unit carefully you will have discovered that this is a complex area of law which clearly needs some reform. The vocabulary is difficult, so have your index cards ready with definitions of all the key words. The Government is planning reform in this area but it has still not arrived. Keep an eye out in the press.

The key piece of legislation remains the **Offences Against the Person Act 1861**. When this was written, it was simply an attempt to collect together some of the legislation that had become scattered. The language, old-fashioned even in 1861, was retained.

Revision checklist

1   Common assault: the accused must have placed the victim in fear of immediate unlawful violence or actually inflicted violence on the victim, *or* the accused intended to put the victim in fear of violence or intended actually to inflict violence on the victim.

2   Assault and battery are two separate offences according to the **Offences Against the Person Act 1861**.

3   The **Criminal Justice Act 1988** seems to bring assault and battery together as one offence in Section 40, but implies they are separate in Section 39.

4   Battery can be indirect, as in *Fagan v Metropolitan Police (1968)* where a car was used by the defendant.

5   An action that results in an actual injury is regarded as more serious by the courts.

6   Assault occasioning actual bodily harm: the accused was responsible for the common assault of the victim that caused actual bodily harm, *or* the accused intended to assault the victim or behaved recklessly so that assault took place and actual bodily harm occurred.

7   Malicious wounding or inflicting grievous bodily harm: the accused must have unlawfully wounded the victim, breaking the whole skin or seriously injured the victim, *or* they must have intended some harm (but not serious harm) or behaved recklessly so that the harm took place (but not serious harm).

8   Malicious wounding or inflicting grievous bodily harm with intent: accused must have unlawfully wounded the victim, breaking the whole skin or seriously injured the victim, *or* they must have intended grievous bodily harm or resisted arrest and have intended or behaved recklessly so that harm took place.

9   Wounding or causing grievous bodily harm with intent is regarded as the most serious non-fatal offence against the person.

10 The Law Commission is currently looking for ways of simplifying words and definitions of the law relating to non-fatal offences and collecting it together in one place.

Quick revision questions

1 What is the *actus reus* of common assault?

2 What is the *mens rea* of common assault?

3 Define *assault*.

4 Define *battery*.

5 Why is *R v Ireland (1997)* an important case?

6 What does the offence 'assault occasioning actual bodily harm' involve?

7 What does the word *occasion* mean?

8 Explain the details of *R v Spratt (1991)* and *R v Savage (1991)*.

9 Define the word *malicious*.

10 What is regarded as the most serious non-fatal offence against a person?

Exam question

1 *a* Outline the key non-fatal offences against the person. (10 marks)

  b Using examples of cases you are familiar with, examine the issues that surround *actus reus* and *mens rea* in non-fatal offences against the person. (20 marks)

Exam answer guide

1 *a* The key offences are:

  ✓ Common assault (formerly assault and battery)

  ✓ Assault occasioning actual bodily harm

  ✓ Malicious wounding/inflicting grievous bodily harm

  ✓ Wounding with intent or causing grievous bodily harm with intent.

  Give a brief description of each.

  b Cases could include:

  ✓ *R v Ireland (1997)*: where assault happened without physical contact using a telephone

  ✓ *DPP v K (a minor) (1990)*: hot-air dryer assault. Again, did not have to be there for assault to have happened

  ✓ *R v Spratt (1991)*: reckless use of an air-rifle.

  ✓ *R v Savage (1991)*: beer glass in pub. *Mens rea* sufficiently proved by fact the defendant threw the beer.

Unit 4

Strict liability

Why do I need to know about strict liability?

Strict liability puts another perspective on the link between *actus reus* and *mens rea*. You will need to understand the situations where limited *mens rea* or even no *mens rea* is sufficient for a successful prosecution. Strict liability remains a controversial area because it does not require a deliberate desire to commit an offence. The areas covered by strict liability include day-to-day activities that affect us all. Questions on strict liability require knowledge of relevant legal cases. This knowledge of cases is also an important aid in understanding and applying this concept.

Strict liability

Strict liability and absolute liability

Strict liability

Strict liability involves offences where the *mens rea* to some elements of the *actus reus* do not have to be proved. The defendant will be found guilty even if they did not mean to commit the offence or did not have a guilty mind for all of their actions.

There are four reasons for strict liability.

● It would be impossible ever to prove the *mens rea* of the defendant in some types of offences.

● There is a greater benefit to the public, even if it may appear a little unfair on the defendant.

● The consequences of the offence would be so serious that a very firm line must be taken.

● Having such an offence as an example makes other people extra careful in their behaviour.

Normally the prosecution must prove the defendant had a guilty mind (*mens rea*) for all of the *actus reus* (the guilty act). *R v Prince (1875)* illustrates the accused committing an act where the prosecution does not have to prove the *mens rea* for at least some elements of the *actus reus*.

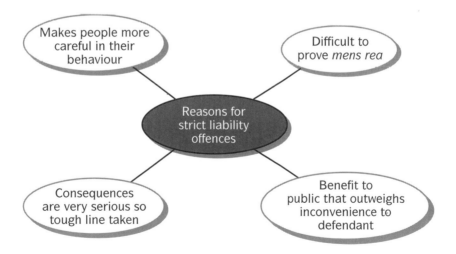

Reasons for strict liability offences

Legal case: R v Prince (1875)

The defendant was found guilty under the **Offences Against the Person Act 1861** when he took a sixteen-year-old girl out of the possession of her father. He believed the girl to be eighteen. The prosecution did not have to prove that the defendant did or did not know the girl was only sixteen, but only that he had taken her from her father. Strict liability applied with regard to the age of the girl and the defendant was found guilty.

The types of offences that are covered by strict liability are often ones that relate to public health or safety, such as food quality, the condition of the car that you drive, speeding offences and parking violations. It would be very difficult to prove *mens rea* in such cases, and so this is dispensed with as a matter of public policy. The benefits seem to outweigh the costs overall.

Pharmaceutical Society of Great Britain v Storkwain (1986) illustrates the seriousness of strict liability cases and the pressures put upon professionals to be absolutely careful in the course of their work.

Legal case: Pharmaceutical Society of Great Britain v Storkwain (1986)

The pharmacist in this case supplied a restricted drug to an addict on a forged prescription. The pharmacist was found guilty of an offence, despite no fault on his part. Strict liability was relevant since he was the one who supplied the drug.

Absolute liability

Some offences do not require any element of *mens rea* to be proved. This is known as *absolute liability*. The only thing that needs proving is the *actus reus*.

Legal case: Winzar v Chief Constable of Kent (1983)

The defendant was taken to hospital on a stretcher but ejected because he was drunk. Later he was found wilting in a seat inside the hospital. The police were called and the defendant was taken outside. The police car was parked on the hospital forecourt. Winzar was found guilty of being drunk on the highway (hospital forecourt). Absolute liability meant he was still guilty, even though he had no part to play in putting himself on the highway.

Absolute liability

Legal case: R v Larsonneur (1932)

The defendant was deported from the Republic of Ireland under police guard. She was arrested at Holyhead when the boat came in and charged with being in the UK without permission. She was eventually convicted of the offence, even though she had no part to play in ending up in the UK. The fact that she was here was enough.

Group activity

Comment on the Winzar and Larsonneur cases. Do you think it was fair that both were convicted of offences when essentially it was the police who put them into the situation they found themselves in?

2   Strict liability and common law

Judges have not been particularly interested in creating strict liability precedents. Very few common law offences do not require *mens rea*. The few that do exist include criminal **libel** and blasphemous libel.

- *Criminal libel:* Editors of newspapers may be held strictly responsible for libellous articles that are published, with or without their knowledge.

- *Blasphemous libel:* This common law offence is once more a topical issue since the attacks on the World Trade Centre. The Government has attempted to bring in changes to the law of blasphemy so that it includes Muslims and other religious believers. Until now the common law offence of blasphemy has only covered Christians. A moral campaigner called Mrs Mary Whitehouse was the last to use it successfully in 1979.

Legal case: Whitehouse v Lemon and Gay News Ltd (1979)

Gay News, a publication of Gay News Ltd, published an illustrated poem which described sexual abuses of Christ after his crucifixion. Mrs Mary Whitehouse brought a private prosecution against the editor, Mr Denis Lemon, for publishing this material. The publication of the blasphemous words meant he was subject to strict liability under this common law.

Criminal contempt of court

Contempt of court is a common law which covers behaviour that interferes with the running of the court system. It can include unruly behaviour in court, such as shouting or being drunk, disobeying the judgment of the court or anything in fact which obstructs the court's work. The old common law of contempt has changed due to the **Contempt of Court Act 1981**, but it remains a strict liability offence.

Jargon buster

Libel involves written lies about a person's character; **slander** involves speech or gestures.

3 Strict liability and statutory law

Statutory law

Most of the strict liability offences are statutory offences. These offences were mostly passed during the nineteenth and twentieth centuries as business and commerce started to expand and there were worries about public safety in a number of areas.

The sale of food to the public

This included shops and restaurants. The way food was produced had changed, and the possibility for contamination and the poisoning of members of the public had increased. Even with this legislation we have in recent times had problems with BSE in cattle, lysteria in cheese and even metal poisoning in bottled water.

Sales of goods to the public

Businesses are not allowed to describe their goods falsely in advertisements or put misleading prices on their goods in the shops. **The Trade Descriptions Act 1968** is a key part of legislation, keeping the standards of service to customers up to scratch.

Health and safety

One of the most important pieces of legislation of recent years is the **Health and Safety at Work Act 1974**. This forces employers to operate a safe working environment, with regular safety checks and the provision of safety equipment and training. Even with these provisions many thousands of people are injured and hundreds killed every year at work.

Presumption of mens rea

For most criminal cases there in a presumption that the prosecution must prove that the accused had some level of *mens rea*. Courts, on the other hand, are prepared to see the legislation as strict liability and do away with the presumption of *mens rea* if the statute states this to be the case or implies it through the wording of the legislation. This is an example of *statutory interpretation*.

Legal case: Callow v Tillstone (1900)

A butcher had contacted a vet for his professional opinion on a piece of meat. The vet stated that the meat was fit for consumption, but this was later found to be untrue. Although the butcher had gone to some trouble to verify the state of the meat, he was still found guilty.

Strict liability covers many areas

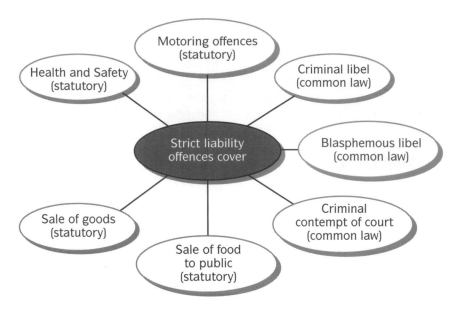

Areas covered by strict liability

The Callow case highlights one of the problems of strict liability. It was presumed that *mens rea* was present, even though the butcher had taken reasonable steps to avoid committing an offence of this nature.

When looking at strict liability cases, some elements of the *actus reus* may require no *mens rea*, while for other elements of the *actus reus* there may be a requirement for *mens rea*, such as intention or negligence. In contrast, absolute liability requires no *mens rea* for any element of the *actus reus*.

Legal case: Sweet v Parsley (1970)

Ms Sweet was a schoolteacher who let rooms to students. The students had the property to themselves for the most part, although Ms Sweet had a room in the house that she used for occasional overnight stops. The students were users of cannabis and other mind-altering drugs. Ms Sweet was convicted under the **Dangerous Drugs Act (1965)** of managing premises for the use of illegal drugs. The case eventually went to the House of Lords, where she won her appeal. The Law Lords decided that direct knowledge of illegal drugtaking on the premises was required.

B v DPP (2000) is a more recent case where the issue of strict liability again highlighted some of the difficulties involved in this legal concept, and also some concerns if strict liability was not used in certain cases. *B v DPP* goes against the trend for assuming strict liability. The consequences could cause concern in some important areas.

Legal case: B v DPP (2000)

The defendant was a fifteen-year-old boy at the time of the offence, and the victim a thirteen-year-old girl. The defendant had committed an illegal sexual act with the girl, but he claimed that he thought she was fourteen or even older. Magistrates hearing the case decided that strict liability applied and convicted the defendant. The Divisional Court supported the magistrates, but the House of Lords eventually quashed the conviction. It ruled that *mens rea* was required as to the age of the child. There would have to be an intention to molest the thirteen-year-old or recklessness as to whether she was under age or not. This could then be linked to the *actus reus* for a conviction.

Group activity

Using the case of *B v DPP*, explore the issues surrounding the use of strict liability in such legal areas. Look at the possible consequences if strict liability was not used and consider the position of the defendant if it is used.

4   Arguments for and against strict liability

This area of law is a controversial one because defendants often feel unfairly treated by the courts, but there are also reasons to keep strict liability offences.

Reasons for keeping strict liability

- The public are protected and reassured that businesses and organizations are striving to make their services clean and safe.

- Businesses and organizations are 'encouraged' to have high standards which benefit the community as a whole.

- Businesses and organizations know exactly where they stand with respect to the law.

- Courts can deal with offences more quickly since the *mens rea* does not have to be proved.

Reasons against keeping strict liability

- The defendant may not consider absence of *mens rea* fair.

- Strict liability might not act as a deterrent, as most businesses are probably keen to have high standards anyway.

- People who otherwise take great care with their actions and have taken all reasonable steps to avoid breaking the law could find themselves in court facing criminal charges.

Revision checklist

1 The prosecution in a strict liability offence does not have to prove all elements of the *mens rea*.

2 The reasons for not having to prove all of the *mens rea* include: difficult if not impossible to prove *mens rea*, benefit to the public, consequences may be very serious, and should improve behaviour since defendant cannot wriggle out of charge.

3 Strict liability is often about public safety, such as selling food or driving a safe car.

4 Strict liability is particularly important to professionals such as pharmacists; see *Pharmaceutical Society of Great Britain v Storkwain (1986)*.

5 Absolute liability requires no *mens rea* to be proved at all.

6 There are not many common law examples of strict liability.

7 Much of strict liability is statutory law covering areas such as sale of food, trading of goods and services, and health and safety.

8 A recent case, *B v DPP (2000)*, shows a move away from assuming strict liability.

9 Reasons for strict liability: public more likely to be protected, businesses and individuals more likely to be kept in line, everyone knows where they stand with the law, and cases dealt with more quickly since *mens rea* not so much of an issue.

10 Reasons against strict liability: defendants feel themselves not treated fairly, businesses keep high standards anyway, and careful law-abiding defendants still found guilty.

Quick revision questions

1 What are strict liability offences?

2 Why do strict liability offences exist?

3 Why is *R v Prince (1875)* an important case?

4 What are the key areas covered by strict liability statutory offences?

5 How does absolute liability come about?

6 Name three common law strict liability offences.

7 What does the *Callow v Tillstone (1900)* case highlight?

8 Name the key details of *Sweet v Parsley (1970)*.

9 Why is *B v DPP (2000)* an important case?

10 Name three reasons for and against strict liability.

Exam question

1 *a* Outline the meaning of the concept of strict liability. (10 marks)

   b Evaluate the effectiveness of strict liability interpretation. (20 marks)

Exam answer guide

1 *a* Strict liability offences involve a different approach to *mens rea*. For at least part of the *actus reus*, no *mens rea* needs to be proved. This is particularly important in cases which affect public health or safety where it would be extremely difficult to prove *mens rea* for part of the *actus reus*.

   b There are pros and cons to the strict liability approach.

Benefits include:

✓ Public more likely to be protected

✓ Businesses and individuals try harder to avoid committing offences

✓ Know where you stand with the law

✓ Cases dealt with more quickly in court.

Costs include:

✓ Defendants feel themselves not treated fairly

✓ Businesses keep high standards anyway

✓ Even those who try hard may still be found guilty.

One the whole, you could say that it would be impossible to run a complex economic society such as ours without strict liability. The number of areas strict liability covers is enormous. The courts would not be able to cope if *mens rea* had to be proved for all of the *actus reus*.

Unit 5

Sentences available to the criminal courts

Why do I need to know about the sentences available to criminal courts?

Principles of sentencing go the heart of the criminal justice system. Information understood in this unit can be used across the syllabus to give depth to questions asked about the criminal justice system, judges, Government funding of legal services and the

Sentences

power of the appeals system. You need to know about present structures and also about the possible impact of the Government-initiated Halliday Report, which has examined the area of sentencing policy.

1 Aims of sentencing

Criminal offences are related to serious anti-social behaviour. The state attempts to deal with this behaviour by using punishment and the threat of punishment to put a stop to criminal activity. Criminal offences are viewed as serious violations of what is commonly agreed to be normal or acceptable behaviour. The punishment of such behaviour has a number of functions. There are two primary schools of thought on punishment, retributive and utilitarian.

The retributive view

Retributive punishment is about punishment for wrongdoing; it is about revenge on behalf of the victim and society. The saying 'An eye for an eye' sums up this approach.

Someone who supports retribution does not primarily look at the circumstances or background of the defendant. Only what the defendant has done is considered. In addition, the more serious the crime, the more severe is the punishment. The retributive school appeals to many people because of its simplicity. The world of retribution is straightforward. The offender is punished severely and does not reoffend. A clear message is sent out to them and to other potential criminals.

The utilitarian view

The utilitarian hopes to see punishment fulfilling a useful purpose for the individual and the community. If an individual can become a more useful member of society, he or she will be less likely to reoffend.

Punishment

In 1990 the Conservative Government produced a White Paper called *Crime, Justice and Protecting the Public*. This paper called for 'just deserts'. This meant that the punishment should fit the crime. Some people have argued against this position, saying that the economic and social standing of the defendant must be taken into consideration. It might be argued that affluent defendants commit different types of crime and may be in a better position to pay fines. The poorer defendant is possibly more likely to commit crimes that attract harsher custodial punishments and may be more likely to default on their repayments. This increases the likelihood of a custodial sentence.

Does punishment work in the long run? The Conservative Party and the Labour Party are now both happy to be seen as 'tough-on-crime', which presumably means more frequent and longer prison sentences.

Deterrence

The view of the retributionist school of thought is that a harsh and uncompromising sentence will send a signal to other potential offenders and deter those who have had to suffer such a punishment from offending again. There are some questions that arise with this system.

- Is punishment the deterrent, or is it the fear of being caught? If an offender believed there was a 98 per cent chance of being caught, but a relatively light sentence, would they still commit the crime?

- Some crimes are really 'one-offs' which the defendant would never commit again. Is it fair in such circumstances to punish harshly? Does it send a signal to others? Is it relevant to others?

- Many serious crimes are ones where the offender is under a great deal of pressure. Can a person think rationally about deterrent punishments in a very tense and emotionally upsetting situation?

- Does the potential offender know what the sentence is? The offender cannot be deterred by something they know nothing about!

There is some evidence that the deterrent effect becomes less powerful for habitual criminals. If an offender has been imprisoned a number of times, the punishment seems to lose its sting. The habitual criminal may become accustomed to a 'criminal

Deterrent?

way of life'. For such a person the fear of a custodial sentence is reduced and the offender sees prison as 'an occupational hazard'.

Younger offenders cause particular concern. If the cycle of crime can be broken early in a person's life, there may be more hope for them and society. The present system has a series of steps that start with a caution or reprimand and rise through fines, probation, and eventually to custodial sentences. Some people argue that a 'short sharp shock' at the outset of criminal behaviour would work as a profound deterrent. This line has been tried in both the United States and the United Kingdom, with poor results. The **Criminal Justice Act 1982** brought these measures in with so-called 'boot camps'. These camps were military-style detention centres with lots of drilling and hard exercise. The 'boot camps' were abandoned in the **Criminal Justice Act 1988**.

Rehabilitation

The aim of rehabilitation is to change the behaviour of offenders. This may happen if:

- offenders see the pain and damage they have caused through their anti-social behaviour
- educational and training facilities have provided an alternative career path for offenders.

This approach is seen as particularly important for young offenders. Inmates may be able to use skills learned in prison for useful employment on release. However, substantial additional resources are required, and prison budgets are not seen as a priority when governments have to make choices about spending.

Although the rehabilitative approach may seem an effective philosophy, there are some criticisms.

- The approach assumes that the problem is with the individual rather than society
- Poorer individuals may be treated more intensively compared to comfortable middle-class offenders who have 'just made a terrible mistake'.
- The process of rehabilitation involves stripping away the privacy of the offender in group-therapy sessions and invasive questioning about background and family life.

Protection of society

The usual method of protecting citizens from violent or dangerous individuals is by long prison sentences. Murder automatically triggers a life sentence. Rape and other crimes of violence also carry long prison sentences on conviction. An offender who commits a second violent or sexual offence automatically receives a life sentence. This has been the result of recent legislation in the **Crime (Sentences) Act 1997**. Given that the cost of keeping a prisoner 'inside' for a year amounts to over £25 000, this is a very expensive way of protecting the public.

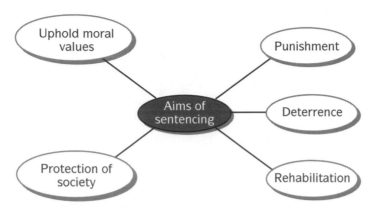

The aims of sentencing

Group activities

1 'Tough on crime and tough on the causes of crime': Tony Blair, Labour Prime Minister.

   'Prison works': Michael Howard, former Conservative Home Secretary.

   a What are the key differences between these two views?

   b How would law and order policies operate under each perspective?

2 'The short, sharp shock': should young offenders be treated more harshly as the **Criminal Justice Act 1982** demanded, or should young offenders be treated more sympathetically, with support and educational facilities? Which approach do you feel has the greatest success in terms of lower reoffending rates in the long run?

3 Many victims and their families applaud the retributive aim. It meets their need for revenge through punishment of the defendant.

   a Do you think retribution is a civilized way to sentence criminals?

   b What factors might a court take into account to give a fairer 'punishment'?

Examination tip

Plan your time. Do not cram at the end.

Custodial sentences

Custodial sentences involve depriving the convicted person of their liberty and freedom. This is the most severe punishment the criminal justice system uses and it has a major impact on the defendant and their family. It is therefore used with care, and all other possibilities are considered first. A court can only pass a custodial sentence when:

- the offence was so serious that the only response could be a custodial sentence

- the case involved violence or a sexual element and it is thought the public needs protection from the defendant.

Details of sentencing are outlined in the **Powers of Criminal Courts (Sentencing) Act 2000** (PCC). This piece of legislation is now the focus for virtually all sentencing by the courts. The judge decides the length of sentence, although there is guidance available. The sentence depends on:

- the seriousness of the offence

- whether the public need protection from the actions of a violent or sexual offender.

The way that an offender is punished is partly dependent on the political party in office. The last Conservative Government believed that prison was a very effective option. The present Labour Government has gone along the same path, leading to record prison populations even though it has toughened up non-custodial options to allow more use. The current view is that punishment should:

- carry messages of deterrence – the current offender and the potential offender should be aware of the stiff penalties for breaking the law

- reflect the seriousness of the crime – a more serious crime should get a more severe punishment.

Mandatory sentences

Some offences carry *mandatory* (compulsory) sentences. The judge has no flexibility in the punishment he or she gives. For example, no matter what the circumstances surrounding the case, every murder conviction carries a compulsory life sentence. The **Crime (Sentences) Act 1997** also provides for a life sentence if two or more serious offences are committed by the defendant.

Concurrent and consecutive sentences

Custodial sentences may be served concurrently or consecutively. *Concurrent* sentences are all served at the same time. Therefore if a series of five offences is carried out which each has a ten-year term, only ten years will be served by the prisoner.

$$10 + 10 + 10 + 10 + 10 = 10$$

Concurrent sentences

If the same five sentences were *consecutive*, then a total of 50 years is served.

$$10 + 10 + 10 + 10 + 10 = 50$$

Consecutive sentences

Community sentences

A custodial sentence is seen as the most severe punishment to be handed down to the offender. Some offences do not require such a harsh penalty. One option available to the courts is a community sentence, which is served in the community and not in prison but does, however, interfere with the offender's day-to-day life. The offender is required to carry out tasks and fulfil certain duties. If not, they can be brought back to court. Community sentences are only possible if the offence may have warranted a prison sentence. There are many types of community sentences.

Community Rehabilitation Order (Probation Order)

The offender is required to see a probation officer regularly for between six months and three years. The probation officer gives guidance to the offender and monitors his or her progress. There may be conditions attached to the probation order which might include:

● the offender living at a particular address

● the offender going for counselling or other medical treatment to support their rehabilitation

● the offender not seeing or communicating with certain people or types of people, possibly including known criminals.

The Government has recently changed the name of a Probation Order to a Community Rehabilitation Order (Section 41, PCC). This clearly signals the hope that the process will reform the offender and change their behaviour.

Unfortunately some offenders see the issue of a Community Rehabilitation Order as a soft option. It is offered instead of prison, so in one sense it is a lot less drastic. The aim, however, is a mix of punishment and rehabilitation. Prison provides a far less effective environment for rehabilitation of the offender.

Community Punishment Order (Community Service Order)

Community Punishment Orders (Section 46, PCC) are meant to carry an element of punishment, but also involve a degree of rehabilitation and also of compensation to the community. The offender is required to carry out tasks such as decorating the homes of the elderly, helping with local environmental projects, and supporting charities and churches with their good works. The name of these orders has changed to underline the punishment element. The total time involved is between 40 and 240 hours.

Community Punishment and Rehabilitation Order (Combination Order)

A Community Punishment and Rehabilitation Orders (Section 51, PCC) is a combination of a punishment order and a rehabilitation order. The offender would have to attend probation interviews to monitor progress and also fulfil some community work.

$$\text{Community Rehabilitation Order} \quad + \quad \text{Community Punishment Order} \quad = \quad \text{Community Punishment and Rehabilitation Order}$$

Curfew Order

Under a Curfew Order, the offender agrees to be at a particular place for an agreed number of hours. Often the offender must be at home between 7pm and 7am. Electronic tagging enforces the order. A tag is attached to the offender's ankle and if he or she moves from the agreed location the police are notified. This is an infringement of liberties, but the alternative is to be held in custody. Given the choice, most offenders go for tagging (Section 37, PCC).

Exclusion Order

Offenders may be banned from certain areas where they have offended or may come in contact with those who may encourage them to offend. Exclusion Orders (Section 40,

The Curfew Order

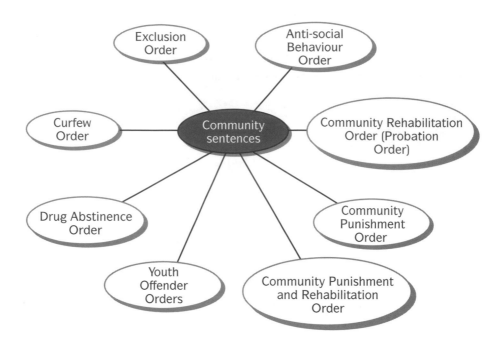

Community sentences

PCC) can last for up to two years if the offender is over sixteen and up to three months if under sixteen.

Anti-social Behaviour Order

The **Crime and Disorder Act 1998** made possible Anti-social Behaviour Orders. These orders are intended for younger offenders aged over ten who indulge in behaviour that causes concern to the local community. Yobbish behaviour and petty vandalism are the normal type of offences. Local authorities or the police seldom use these orders. There seem to be major problems about their enforcement and their effectiveness.

Drug Abstinence Order

Drug Abstinence Orders (Section 56, PCC) apply to class A drugs such as heroin. The offender is formally banned from taking these drugs for between six months and three years. The order is there to emphasize to the offender the will of the court in a more obvious way. Taking class A drugs is, of course, illegal at any time, other than for authorized medical purposes.

Young offenders and sentencing

Clearly, courts are keen to impose community sentences rather than custodial sentences for young people. There are a variety of Community Orders that can be applied to young offenders.

Action Plan

The young offender has to become involved in set activities or avoid certain locations (Section 69, PCC).

Referral

The young offender may have to meet with a Youth Offending team to get advice and guidance.

Parental Order

Parents/guardians can be ordered to take full responsibility for the offender for up to three years (Section 150, PCC) and forced to attend counselling sessions to support them. If they do not comply then they face court action themselves.

Children under ten

Children under ten cannot be held criminally responsible, but there are powers to deal with them if they commit criminal offences. They can be put under the supervision of a social worker or forced to see a member of the Youth Offending team. They can also be ordered to stay away from certain locations and to be kept indoors for certain times of the day or night; this is called a *curfew*.

Young offenders

Group activity

Murder carries a life sentence, no matter what the circumstances of the case and regardless of the personal circumstances of the defendant.

1 Can you think of some examples where the judge should be given some flexibility over the sentence they pass?

2 What benefits come from having one sentence for all?

Research activity

Explore the statistics for the prison population on the Home Office website www.homeoffice.gov.uk and the HM Prisons site www.hmprisonservice.gov.uk and see if you can identify any trends in totals and within the different groups.

Revision card activity

Make a set of revision cards showing the key elements of community-based sentencing.

3 Fines

When a court orders an offender to pay money as punishment for their crime, the money is paid to the state. The victim of the crime does not receive it. If money is paid to the victim, it is known as a Compensation Order.

A problem arises when deciding what level of fine to impose. The personal financial circumstances of the offender can make a significant difference. A custodial sentence would affect both in roughly the same way, but a fine might be of much less importance to a very rich person than to a poor person. In relative terms the poor person would have been punished much more harshly than the rich person. If a fine is going to work as a punishment, then the richer person should pay a much higher penalty. On the other hand, a person on Income Support who only has £40 per week to live on should expect a much smaller fine. The **Criminal Justice Act 1993** abolished the system that hoped to deal with this situation because of the many problems that arose.

The level of fines appropriate for each offence is listed in the legislation. It is up to magistrates and judges to use their common sense when applying the punishment to offenders.

Fines — no problem for some

4 | Discharges

Absolute discharge

If the court is satisfied that no punishment is appropriate, then it may give an absolute discharge. This means that the offender is free to go and is not subject to any conditions.

An absolute discharge is given in circumstances when the offender has pleaded guilty or is found guilty. The court records the offence but nothing else happens to the offender. Absolute discharges are rare. They often involve cases where people have committed a criminal offence but have had strong justifying reasons to do so.

Conditional discharge

It is much more likely that the court will apply some conditions to the offender if they are released without formal punishment. The most common is that they are *bound over*. This means that if they commit another offence within a set time period (normally up to three years) the offender will be brought to court to face the new charges and the old ones again.

Jargon buster

Crimes caused by an unusual situation may have this factor taken into account. The situation is known as an *extenuating* or *mitigating circumstance*.

5 Compensation

As mentioned earlier, fines go to the state rather than the victim. There is, however, a method of forcing the offender to compensate their victim. This is known as a Compensation Order (Section 130, PCC). These can be imposed in addition to, or instead of, a custodial or community sentence. Compensation Orders are an attempt at reparation (repair for the damage done) for the victim.

Group activity

Recent guidelines advise that the following amounts be given to victims between 20 and 35 years old in compensation for injury. More can be paid to older people.

Graze: up to £50
Bruise: up to £75
Black eye: £100
Cut without scarring: £75–500
Loss of a tooth: £250–500 (£1000 for a front tooth)
Broken nose: £750–1750
Fractured jaw: £2750

Comment on the amounts awarded.

6 Other powers

The mentally ill

The courts also have powers to deal with offenders who are mentally ill. It would be inappropriate to use normal sentencing powers on people suffering from mental illnesses.

- Treatment orders: the offender may be required to receive treatment from their doctor or from the out-patient department of a hospital as part of the conditions of their release from the court.

- Hospital orders: the offender is ordered to attend a hospital as an in-patient to receive appropriate treatment.

- Secure hospitals: if the offender is believed to be dangerous to themselves or others, they may be detained under Section 41 of the **Mental Health Act 1983** and held in a secure hospital.

Awards from public funds

One last power the courts have is to award small gifts of money to members of the public if they have acted in a particularly heroic or community-minded manner. The usual payment is £50 or £100. Local newspapers often tell the tale.

7 Sentencing and reoffending rates

Reoffending rates

Sentencing should have an impact on crime in several different ways.

- Deterrence should be sharper and more effective.

- Imprisonment should reduce levels of serious crime as criminals are in jail and not on the street.

- Reform and rehabilitation should be producing potential reoffenders who consider their victims and resist offending again.

- Reparation, where victims get compensation from the offender, should discourage some potential criminals.

It is not, however, a rosy picture. What happens when we look at reoffending rates? It might be more accurate to talk about *reconviction* rather than reoffending rates since there is no evidence if reoffenders are not caught. There are some alarming findings in the statistical evidence.

Length of sentence and reconviction rates

Seventy per cent of all offenders released in 1987 offended again within five years. However, the following differences in reconviction were shown in the statistics (*Prison Statistics, England and Wales, 1999*).

Reconviction rates were higher for those serving shorter sentences than for those serving longer sentences. Those reconvicted within two years of discharge in 1996 were:

- sentence up to twelve months: 60 per cent

- sentence over twelve months but less than four years: 53 per cent

- sentence over four years but less than ten years: 31 per cent

- sentence over ten years but less than life imprisonment: 29 per cent

- life sentence: 5 per cent.

Age and reconviction rates

Age is another factor which determines the level of reconviction rates. The following evidence suggests a strong relationship. Reconviction rates within two years for males released in 1996 were:

- 14–16 year-olds: 85 per cent

- 17–20 year-olds: 74 per cent

- above 20 years-old: 76 per cent.

These figures are particularly worrying. If younger offenders are returning to young offender institutions or prisons, a pattern is being set which may prove difficult to break out of.

The costs of long-term custodial sentences are astronomic. A prisoner who spends fifteen years in prison will cost the taxpayer approximately £375 000. There are clearly better ways to spend the money.

Nature of crime and reconviction rates

The statistics indicate that offenders imprisoned for certain types of offences have a much higher reconviction rate than others. In 1996 the following rates for reconviction within two years were:

- burglary: 76 per cent

- theft and handling: 71 per cent

- robbery: 55 per cent

- fraud and forgery: 24 per cent

- sexual offences: 19 per cent.

These figures, of course, cross-reference with age of offender and length of sentence, so the picture can be difficult to put together.

Revision card activity

Make notes of the key figures in the reconviction statistics supplied by *Prison Statistics*.

Research activity

Using the statistics on length of sentence, age of offender and nature of the offence, give reasons for the variations in reconviction rates.

8 Halliday Report and reform

A major review into the effects of punishments was published in July 2001. The Halliday Report investigated the effectiveness of the sentencing framework for England and Wales. It attempted to suggest improvements into what were perceived by many as unsatisfactory current arrangements.

In all there were 55 major recommendations, including:

- the targeting of persistent offenders

- research into the contribution of sentencing to crime reduction

- increasing the severity of the sentence when the offender has recent convictions

- using imprisonment only as a last resort

- a review of mandatory minimum sentences so that judges could have more sentencing flexibility.

The Report's author, John Halliday, concludes that the present use of short prison sentences is not working and that the problem of persistent offenders is not being adequately tackled.

The Halliday Report

Group activity

The prison population (England and Wales) on 23 November 2001 was:

53 779 adult male prisoners

3469 adult female prisoners

10 539 male offenders between the ages of 15 and 21

570 female offenders between the ages of 15 and 21

68 357 in total.

1 How do you account for the numbers and the differences between the groups?

2 Do you think the trends will change over the next twenty years?

Web activity

The Halliday Report contains a vast array of data and charts on the effects of sentencing policy. See the full document on the Home Office website at www.homeoffice.gov.uk/cpd/sou/sfrleaft.

Revision checklist

1 Aims of sentencing include: punishment, deterrence, rehabilitation, protection of society and reparation.

2 Seventy per cent of offenders are reconvicted within five years.

3 Those serving shorter sentences are more likely to be reconvicted.

4 Younger offenders more likely to reoffend.

5 The main community sentences are: Community Rehabilitation Orders, Community Punishment Orders and Community Punishment and Rehabilitation Orders.

6 Other powers of the court include Curfew Orders, Exclusion Orders, Anti-social Behaviour Orders and Drug Abstinence Orders.

7 The court has powers to order the treatment of mentally ill offenders or even to put them into secure hospitals.

8 There are powers to compel parents/guardians to take responsibility for their children or face court action.

9 Fines are paid to the state and not to the victim of the offence. They may penalize the poor more than the rich.

10 Victims of crime can receive compensation via Compensation Orders.

Quick revision questions

1 What is a criminal offence?

2 What are the two views on sentencing and punishment?

3 What are the main aims of sentencing?

4 What was the 'short, sharp shock'?

5 What is the difference between a consecutive and a concurrent sentence?

6 What are the main types of community sentence?

7 Why do fines penalize the poor unfairly?

8 What is a conditional discharge?

9 What is a Compensation Order?

10 What Act of Parliament allows the secure detention of a mentally ill person?

Exam question

1 a What sentences do courts have at their disposal? (10 marks)

 b What sentences are most effective in preventing the reconviction of offenders? (20 marks)

Exam answer guide

1 a The key sentences courts have at their disposal include:

✓ Custodial

✓ Community sentences

✓ Fines

✓ Curfews, Exclusion Orders and Drug Abstinence Orders

✓ Absolute and conditional discharges.

Give a brief description of each. You do not have time to evaluate each so move quickly onto part **b**, which requires more time and asks for higher-level skills to be demonstrated.

 b This part of the question is asking you for an opinion. Choose two or three of your answers to **a** and develop points around the effectiveness of each. Support your points with arguments and any statistics you are able to give. The examiner is looking for thoughtful and analytical arguments followed by a reasoned conclusion.

Unit 6 Tort

Why do I need to know about tort?

Tort covers a wide range of legal topics, but the area you will specialize in on this syllabus will be the tort of negligence. Questions will require you to understand the basic principles of tort and apply legal cases to support your arguments. Look at the diagrams on negligence and duty of care to get an overview of how everything fits together. The subject can be challenging, so break concepts down using revision cards wherever you can. Examiners are keen to see that students understand the basic concepts thoroughly and can use cases to back up their points.

Tort

1 Definition of tort

Tort is part of civil law. It involves compensating a victim who has been wronged in some way. Examples of the law of tort include the following:

- Suing a hospital which has made a mistake and injured the patient – A young man recently died after being given the wrong injection by tired and inexperienced junior hospital doctors.

- Taking action against an employer who allows an unsafe working environment for employees – A 39-year-old man working at a frozen-food company took action using tort. He had been hit by a heavy metal beam which fell and broke his back, leaving him paralysed.

- Protecting land against trespassers – The Ramblers Association, which tries to keep countryside pathways open, are now experts at defending cases of tort taken against them by large landowners.

- Preventing a nuisance such as loud music – More powerful music systems and houses and flats built with insufficient sound insulation have led to a huge increase in claims of nuisance.

- Compensation for a financial loss if there has been some misleading information given. If a bank gives a credit reference which is incorrect, they may be liable to action if someone else loses money as a result.

The noise nuisance

Tort does not for the most part involve punishing the wrongdoer. It is not about proving guilt. Instead, it attempts to find a **remedy**, and compensate the victim of the wrongdoing. It tries to put the claimant back into the same position they were in before the wrong was committed. If the court feels that the defendant should pay money to compensate the victim, it is often referred to as **damages**.

Each of the above must have an additional element. It must attract liability in law. Someone must be responsible for the event which has led to the injury.

Tort and criminal law

Tort is concerned with finding the person who is liable (rather than guilty) for the event for which a claimant is seeking compensation. In many cases a person does not intentionally create the wrong. A doctor making a mistake because they are tired does not deliberately attempt to injure the patient. The employer did not put a faulty piece of machinery that harmed an employee there on purpose. Tort attempts to put things right for the victim, not to punish the defendant.

Standard of proof

Another difference between tort and criminal law is the standard of proof needed to win a case. In a criminal case the prosecution must prove their case 'beyond a reasonable doubt'. In a tort case they must find someone liable 'on the balance of probabilities'. This is much easier to prove. The key reasons for the difference in these levels of proof are the consequences. A criminal case may result in a custodial sentence and a criminal record for the defendant. A tort case will result in the payment of some compensation by the defendant.

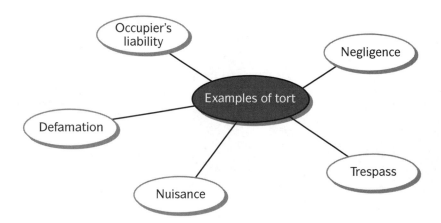

Examples of tort

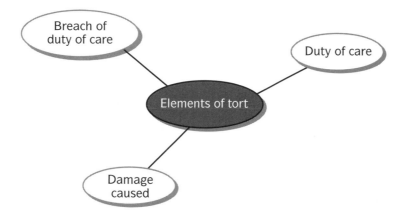

Elements of tort

Categories of tort

There are a variety of torts which the court can hear. They include:

- negligence – failure to be careful

- trespass to the person – failure to respect other individuals

- nuisance – failure to respect the rights of neighbours

- defamation – failure to respect the good name of others

- occupier's liability – failure to take care of visitors (and even trespassers).

Jargon buster

- The French word **tort** means 'a wrong'.

- **Remedies** are used in tort cases and civil cases. They are the 'sentence' of the court on the losing defendant and often take the form of money paid in compensation.

- **Damage** and **damages** are two separate issues. The first involves injury or destruction, while the second is compensation for a wrong done to a claimant.

Revision card activity

Using index cards note the key areas of tort.

2 | Aims of tort

There are two main aims associated with tort: compensation and deterrence.

Compensation

The law of tort tries to put the victim back to where they were before the incident. Clearly this is very difficult in a case that involves physical injury or a trauma that has affected the victim's psychological well-being. The most that can be hoped for in the majority of cases is that the victim feels that 'justice has been done' in some way by the payment of damages.

Deterrence

It would be generally accepted that the best situation is to have no wrongdoings and no tort cases. Everybody loses, in a sense. A wrongdoing has been suffered and damages have been paid. Another key aim of the law of tort is to change the behaviour of people so that the circumstances leading to cases are reduced. This is known as *deterrence*. It is hoped that if a potential wrongdoer knows that compensation has to be paid, they will take more care. If more care and attention are paid, the scope for accidents and mistakes is reduced.

3 | Tort of negligence and duty of care

The tort of negligence involves wrongdoers paying compensation for damage they have caused. We must first establish what the word *negligence* means. In law it is defined as

> 'a failure to act in a reasonable way when you have a duty of care towards another person.'

If this is the case, the victim may be entitled to compensation. The concept of negligence is a difficult one and has been broken into three separate parts:

● Duty of care owed by the defendant to the claimant

● Breach of that duty of care

● Damage caused to the claimant as a result of the defendant's breach in duty of care.

All three parts have to be present before negligence can be proved.

The concept of *liability* is an important one when discussing a breach of duty of care. Liability exists where there is a legal obligation from one party to another.

Duty of care

There are many occasions in ordinary life when people are negligent. Not all, however, end up as legal cases. One requirement for proving the tort of negligence is that a duty

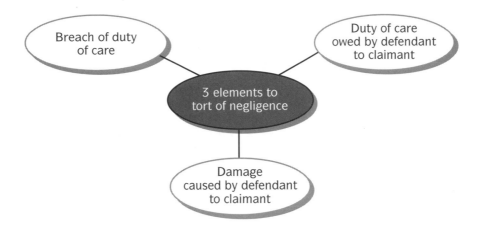

Elements of tort of negligence

of care exists between the claimant and defendant. It is the duty of the court to decide whether there is a duty of care and whether liability exists if something goes wrong. Duty of care is explained further in Module 3 Unit 7.

One of the most famous cases in the tort of negligence is *Donoghue v Stevenson (1932)*.

Legal case: Donoghue v Stevenson (1932)

This case established the modern tort of negligence. The claimant had gone to a café with a friend and bought some ginger beer in a dark bottle. The claimant drank some of the beer, and when she poured the remains into the glass found a decomposed snail. As she had drunk much of the beer, this made her feel sick. She successfully sued the manufacturer using the tort of negligence.

The *Donoghue v Stevenson* case established important principles in the tort of negligence. Lord Atkins was the judge in the case. Part of his judgment included the following:

> 'You must take reasonable care to avoid acts or omissions which you can reasonably foresee would be likely to injure persons who are closely and directly affected by your acts.'

Duty of care and the 'neighbour test'

The 'neighbour test' was created by Lord Atkins to explore whether a duty of care was present. If by using common sense the defendant could see that an action or omission could lead to the harm of another person, then a duty of care is owed.

Duty of care and the three-part test

There is a more modern three-part test used when attempting to prove duty of care. It arose from the case of *Carparo Industries v Dickman (1990)*.

The neighbour

Legal case: Carparo Industries v Dickman (1990)

The case involved the claimants suing a firm of accountants for supplying false information. The claimants wanted to buy a company and based their wish to do so on the annual accounts of the company, which showed £1.3 million profit. When the transaction was complete they found that the true picture was in fact a £465 000 loss. They blamed the firm of accountants for their misfortune. The court decided that the accountants did not owe a duty of care to Carparo Industries.

The three-part test consists of three questions.

1 Was the damage foreseeable?

A reasonable person driving at 60 miles per hour through a built-up urban area should be able to foresee the possibility of seriously injuring or even killing someone. Someone having common sense and acting upon it presumably would not drive so carelessly. Often when looking at a case we need to look no further than asking ourselves the question 'did the defendant use common sense?'

2 Was there sufficient proximity between claimant and defendant?

The case of *Anns v Merton LBC (1977)* produced the following question from Lord Wilberforce. It concerned the relationship between claimant and defendant if a duty of care was to be proved:

'One has to ask whether there is a sufficient relationship of proximity or neighbourhood between the alleged wrongdoer and the person who has suffered damage to prove a duty of care exists?'

In other words, are the two sides adequately connected to the extent that the defendant's actions or omissions would attract liability for damages to the claimant?

3 Is it fair and just to create a duty of care between the claimant and defendant?

In *Anns v Merton LBC (1977)* Lord Wilberforce also argued that it was necessary:

'to consider whether there were any considerations which ought to negate or limit the scope of the duty or the class of person to whom a duty of care is owed.'

The judges were allowing themselves some flexibility to come to a just decision if they thought the defendant was being unfairly asked to shoulder a duty of care.

A fourth question has arisen over the course of time as a consequence of the third question in the three-part test.

4 Are there any public policy issues that would make such a duty of care a serious problem?

The jobs of police, fire brigade, ambulance service, doctors, nurses and teachers would be incredibly difficult if they were constantly hauled before the courts to answer for their work. In some extreme cases this does of course happen, but courts tend to discourage these civil actions.

Hill v Chief Constable of West Yorkshire Police (1988) was an important case connected to duty of care involving public servants.

Three-part test for duty of care: Carparo Industries v Dickman (1990)

Legal case: Hill v Chief Constable of West Yorkshire Police (1988)

The mother of the last victim of the serial murderer Peter Sutcliffe (known as the Yorkshire Ripper) took action against the Chief Constable of West Yorkshire Police for failing to catch the murderer before her daughter became a victim. Mrs Hill believed that the Chief Constable's officers had been negligent. They had interviewed Peter Sutcliffe during their enquiries but had not uncovered any clear evidence against him. They had in fact interviewed hundreds of suspects in their enquiries. The mother lost the case on the basis that a duty of care, in a legal sense, had not been established.

Revision checklist

1 Tort is part of civil law.
2 Tort involves compensating those claimants who have been wronged. It is not intended as a method of punishing the defendant.
3 The standard of proof required in tort is based on the balance of probabilities.
4 Areas covered by tort include: negligence, trespass, nuisance, defamation, and occupier's liability.
5 The two main aims of tort are: compensation and deterrence.
6 Tort involves proving negligence, which can be defined as: a failure to act in a reasonable way when you have a duty of care towards another person.
7 There are three elements needed to prove negligence: duty of care, breach of duty and damage caused.
8 Duty of care involves three questions: Was the incident foreseen by the defendant? Was there a reasonably strong relationship between claimant and defendant? Is it fair to create a duty of care between claimant and defendant? A fourth question has arisen over time concerning public servants and the duty of care they owe people they serve.
9 The case of *Donoghue and Stevenson (1932)* was an important case in the development of tort negligence.
10 The questions in *Carparo Industries v Dickman (1990)* are used to explore duty of care, along with *Anns v Merton LBC (1977)*.

Quick revision questions

1 List three examples of tort.

2 What is the relationship between criminal law and tort?

3 What is the difference between *damage* and *damages*?

4 What is liability?

5 What are the two main aims of tort?

6 What does deterrence hope to achieve?

7 Define the tort of negligence.

8 What is the three-part test?

9 How was the *Anns v Merton LBC (1977)* case used?

10 What public policy issues might arise concerning tort of negligence and the police?

Exam question

1 *a* Distinguish between criminal law and the law of tort. (15 marks)

   b What are the main problems facing a claimant when taking a case to court?
        (15 marks)

Exam answer guide

1 *a* The key differences between criminal law and the law of tort are:

   ✓ Criminal law attempts to punish, tort does not

   ✓ Criminal law requires a much higher degree of proof than tort

   ✓ Criminal law attempts to find guilt, tort attempts to find liability

   ✓ Criminal law may involve prison and a criminal record, tort is about righting a
     wrong and putting the claimant back where they were.

   b The claimant has a number of difficulties including:

   ✓ Proving a duty of care

   ✓ Claimant can use the three-part test

   ✓ Event that causes damage must be reasonably foreseeable

   ✓ Claimant and defendant must have a reasonably close relationship

   ✓ The court must decide that it is fair to impose a duty of care

   ✓ Public policy makes it difficult to sue public servants such as police officers,
     firefighters or doctors.

Breach of duty of care

Key points

1   Breach of duty of care
2   Damage caused by the defendant
3   Remoteness
4   Remedies in tort

Why do I need to know about breach of duty of care?

Breach of duty of care goes to the heart of questions on negligence. Without an understanding of breach of duty of care you will struggle to answer questions on tort. Always break down concepts in this area to aid your understanding. Go slowly and look back at what you have already covered to illuminate what you are working on. When reading this unit, remember that *damage* and *damages* are two separate concepts. The first refers to the result of the negligence, the second to compensation for the negligence. Using index cards thoughtfully will assist you greatly on the topic of tort.

Whoops!

1 Breach of duty of care

Remember once again the elements that have to be present for negligence:

1 Duty of care owed by the defendant to the claimant.

2 Breach of that duty of care owed to the claimant by the defendant.

3 Damage caused to the claimant as a result.

The first element, duty of care, is established using the *Carparo Industries v Dickman (1990)* case and the three-part test. This was explored in the previous unit.

Use of the reasonable man

An *objective test* is used to determine whether the defendant exercised reasonable care. This is a measure of the degree of care a **reasonable man** would have exercised in the same situation. The reasonable man is expected to have ordinary levels of skill and knowledge. He does not have to be an expert.

However, if a person does claim specialist skill they will be compared to a reasonably competent person in that field. A builder who installs a dangerously steep staircase that leads to injury will be compared to a reasonably competent carpenter, but not to Carpenter of the Year.

The man in the street and the objective test

Bolam v Friern Barnet Hospital (1957) illustrates the notion of what is reasonable in the case of a person with professional skills.

Legal case: **Bolam v Friern Barnet Hospital (1957)**

The *Bolam v Friern Barnet Hospital (1957)* case established the Bolam Principle. The doctor at the heart of this medical case was not liable if he 'exercises the ordinary skill of an ordinary competent man exercising that particular art'. He only had to possess the level of skill a reasonably competent doctor would possess. This principle was later applied to a range of professionals.

The wider picture

When judging cases the courts take a number of other factors into account to give a better picture of the events and their wider context.

Degree of risk

If people attempted to avoid all risk, life would not be worth living. Every human action involves some possibility of an awful accident. Even walking downstairs in the morning has its perils. There are some risks created by potential defendants that are so small that they should perhaps be given some flexibility, as in *Bolton v Stone (1951)*.

The risk: going downstairs

Legal case: Bolton v Stone (1951)

A cricket ground was sited next to a road. The owners of the ground recognized that there was a risk of injury if a cricket ball was ever hit out of the ground and onto the road. They took the precaution of erecting fences five metres high around the site. The claimant was 90 metres from the wicket and 65 metres from the fence. The club was found not liable for the injuries to Mrs Bolton. Lord Reid said during the case, however, that the risk and the consequences should be considered.

Seriousness of potential harm

If the potential harm or injury is very serious, individuals and organizations must exercise considerable care to avoid liability for accidents. *Paris v Stepney Borough Council (1951)* illustrates the concern.

Legal case: Paris v Stepney Borough Council (1951)

The claimant, Mr Paris, was blind in one eye. His employer, Stepney Borough Council, asked him to do a job that involved a very small risk to his other eye and provided no protective eyewear. The worst did happen, and Mr Paris was blinded in his one working eye. The accident therefore left him completely blind. His employer was found negligent and ordered to pay compensation.

Cost of precaution

There are times when to try to completely solve a problem would lead to a ridiculous result. The costs would clearly have outweighed any potential benefits in *Latimer v AEC Ltd (1952)*.

Legal case: Latimer v AEC Ltd (1952)

The claimant was injured when he slipped on an oily floor in a factory. The defendant had attempted to minimize risk by putting sawdust on the slippery surface. Lord Denning stated that the defendant had fulfilled his duty of care by his actions, and the only way to avoid all risk would have been to close the factory down. This was not a sensible alternative.

Importance of the risky activity

The court may consider a different approach if the activity under question involved a socially useful purpose. This may often occur when the police are involved, as in *Marshall v Osmand (1982)*. They may be attempting to carry out their lawful duty but be put in the position where risks need to be taken.

Legal case: Marshall v Osmand (1982)

The claimant was involved in stealing a car and was a passenger in the vehicle at the time of arrest. A high-speed car chase occurred, during which the claimant was injured. The court came to the view that police officers doing their jobs did not owe the same duty of care to a fleeing suspect as they would to a law-abiding citizen. The police officer was found not liable for negligence. The Court of Appeal felt the same duty of care should have been given to the suspect, but again the police officer was not negligent.

Proof of breach

It is the task of the claimant to prove that a breach of duty of care has occurred. They must prove this 'beyond the balance of probabilities', which may be very difficult. If this is the case, the claimant may claim that 'the facts speak for themselves' or *res ipsa loquitor*. If this approach is to be used, two criteria must be met:

● The accident that occurred must normally have a negligence element to it.

● The circumstances must directly point to negligence on the part of the defendant.

The principle was established in *Byrne v Boadle (1863)* and *Scott v London and St Catherine Dock Co (1865)*. The first case involved the claimant being hit by a bag of flour falling from the window of a shop. The second involved the claimant being hit by a bag of sugar which fell from a warehouse crane.

Learners and professionals

Learners

A complication arises when the court is faced with a person who is a learner. They may well lack the skills of an ordinary qualified person. A student teacher might not ruin your life, but a learner driver might. The courts have taken the position that they must treat the defendant by the same standards as a qualified person. This is illustrated by *Nettleship v Weston (1971)* and *Wilsher v Essex Health Authority (1987)*.

Legal case: Nettleship v Weston (1971)

A learner driver was involved in a case of negligent driving. Lord Denning stated that the law required him to have 'the same standard of care as any other driver'. The court recognized that the learner driver was not at fault in a moral way, but the interests of the other road users had to be taken into account. If the driver was clearly not up to the job, he should not be driving on a public road.

Legal case: Wilsher v Essex Area Health Authority (1987)

A junior doctor caring for a young child placed a blood oxygen monitor in a vein rather than in an artery. As a result the child received too much oxygen. It was discovered later that the child had severe eye problems. The oxygen was only one of a number of factors that might have been responsible. The case ended with no damages payable since the link could not definitely be proved.

The judge in the case of *Wilsher v Essex Area Health Authority (1987),* however, stated that the patient's expectations of an appropriate level of skill for the task should not be reduced, even considering the pressures faced by young and inexperienced doctors. This case is used later to illustrate 'damage caused'.

Professionals

People who call themselves 'professionals' normally owe their clients a duty of care. Some, like architects and surveyors, insure themselves against the possibility of a legal liability. Some, like teachers, join trade unions, which they hope will sufficiently protect them against complaints or legal action. *Rondel v Worsley (1969)* and *Hall v Simons (2000)* looked at the responsibility a barrister owed his client for work performed.

Legal case: Rondel v Worsley (1969)

It might be thought that a barrister owed a duty of care to his client, particularly given the importance of the outcome to the client. If negligence could be proved, would the barrister be liable? This case stated that this was not the case. The position was taken that barristers would be taken to court every time someone did not like the verdict handed down by a jury, so they deserved a special position. Barristers were immune.

The position has since changed on the ruling given *in Rondel v Worsley* as the result of *Hall v Simons (2000).*

Legal case: Hall v Simons (2000)

Hall v Simons meant that barristers were now open to charges of negligence and could be sued in the civil court. It also meant that barristers could sue for their fees from clients they represented. The House of Lords used the **Practice Statement 1966** to overrule its own previous position.

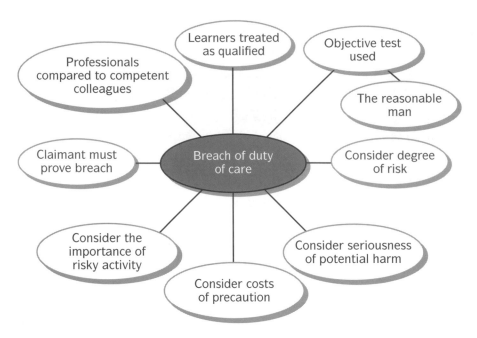

Breach of duty of care – points to consider

Jargon buster

The **reasonable man** is also known as 'the man in the street' or, in older books, as the 'man on the Clapham Omnibus' (tram). This is the *objective test*.

Examination tip

If a case is used to support a point, it must be properly linked to your main strand of argument.

---

2 | Damage caused by the defendant

You saw at the start of this unit that a negligence claim needs to prove duty of care, breach of duty of care and damage caused by the defendant. This section will look at the third element: damage caused by the defendant. If the defendant has not caused the damage, they are not liable for payment of compensation. The victim often has problems in proving this element of negligence.

The test used to see whether damage was caused by the defendant is the 'but for' test:

● But for the defendant's negligence, would the damage have been caused?

A famous case, *Barnett v Chelsea and Kensington Hospital Management Committee (1969),* illustrates the 'but for' test.

Legal case: Barnett v Chelsea and Kensington Hospital Management Committee (1969)

Three night watchmen drank some tea at 5.00am one morning. Soon afterwards all began to feel ill and arrived at hospital at around 8.00am, where they were seen by a nurse. One of the night watchmen, Mr Barnett, was particularly unwell. The doctor was contacted by the nurse but he was himself unwell and told the nurse to send the men off to their own doctors. They all left the hospital. Mr Barnett died at 2.00pm that day.

The widow of Mr Barnett proved a duty of care and that a breach of that duty had occurred. It was later found, however, that all the men had been poisoned by arsenic in their tea. Mr Barnett had died from that cause, not from the breach of duty of the nurse and doctor: 'but for' them he still would have died. Mrs Barnett received no compensation. The verdict given by the Coroner was murder by person or persons unknown.

More than one cause of damage

Another problem for the victim occurs if there is more than one possibility concerning the cause of the damage. The courts have been reluctant to declare liability in these cases. In the *Wilsher v Essex Area Health Authority (1987)* case, the fact that the baby could have suffered damage in more than one way meant the inexperienced junior doctor was not found negligent. It could not be proved that it was him and him alone that caused the damage.

Break in the chain of events

There are also times when there is a break in the chain of events between the negligent act and the damage caused. If this is so, the defendant may not be liable in some cases and be liable in others. Consider the two cases *Performance Cars Ltd v Abraham (1962)* and *Carslogie Steamship Co Ltd v Royal Norweigan Government (1952)*.

Legal case: Performance Cars Ltd v Abraham (1962)

The defendant escaped liability for damage caused to a Rolls Royce because someone had already hit the car in the same place. A respray was already needed because of the first accident. The first accident wiped out liability for the second accident.

Legal case: Carslogie Steamship Co Ltd v Royal Norwegian Government (1952)

A ship was damaged due to the negligence of the defendant. The damaged ship was patched up awaiting a more permanent repair and sent on its way across the Atlantic. It was then damaged by a storm and when at last it got home spent 51 days in dry dock being repaired. Without the storm, the ship would have spent ten days in dry dock being repaired from the defendant's original damage. The defendant escaped liability for the loss of use of the ship during this time because the storm would have meant that it needed a 51-day repair anyway. In this case the second situation wiped out liability for the accident.

3 Remoteness

Another obstacle for the victim is that the damage must have been reasonably foreseeable. The most famous case in this area is known as the *Wagon Mound* case.

Legal case: Overseas Tankship (UK) Ltd v Morts Dock & Engineering Co, the Wagon Mound (1961)

A ship known as *SS Wagon Mound* was refuelling in Sydney Harbour. Oil was negligently spilt into the sea during this process. The ship eventually finished refuelling and sailed away. Oil drifted towards some workers on a wharf who were welding another ship. The welders were told to continue working as the oil would not be ignited by the welding torches being used. Unfortunately a piece of molten metal fell on some cotton waste which in turn set fire to the oil. The ship that was being worked on was damaged, as well as the wharf she was moored to. The owners of the *SS Wagon Mound* were found not liable since these events were not reasonably foreseeable.

Hughes v Lord Advocate (1963) shows the importance of the end result, even if the exact series of events was not foreseeable. The *Wagon Mound* case involves a series of events that were quite unusual and would have been difficult to foresee. A child being burned was not so unlikely.

Legal case: Hughes v Lord Advocate (1963)

Workmen left a manhole open and put paraffin lamps nearby to warn of the danger. A ten-year-old boy playing nearby knocked one of the lamps down the hole, causing an explosion which burned him. The court took the position that it was foreseeable that a child might be burned by one of the lamps, even if the unusual sequence of events which actually caused the burns could not have been easily predicted. Hughes was awarded damages.

If a tort is proved, the defendant has to compensate the claimant. This is known as a *remedy*. There are a number of remedies that are available for the court to choose from.

Damages

Damages means the payment of compensation. This is intended to put the claimant back into the position they were in before the tort had been committed. This is, of course, very artificial. The payment of compensation is not intended to punish the defendant. There are a number of different types of damages that can be awarded.

- **General damages** are paid for the pain, suffering and loss of amenity caused to the claimant. Amenity includes skills people take for granted, such as walking a reasonable distance and being able to use both hands effectively. These are difficult sums to calculate and judges are therefore given help and guidance from the Judicial Studies Board.

- **Special damages** include loss of earnings and medical bills. These damages will normally have paperwork to prove them, so calculation is far easier. The only real problem is trying to predict loss of earnings in the future. This is problematic since rates of recovery from injuries will vary in different individuals.

- **Contemptuous damages** are awarded if the court is unhappy that the case was ever brought before it.

- **Nominal damages** are awarded if the court believes that no real damage has happened, but the claimant's rights have been infringed in some way.

- **Exemplary damages** are awarded to provide a deterrent effect for others.

Injunctions

An *injunction* restrains a defendant from repeating their action. If the injunction is ignored, this is contempt of court and the defendant can be arrested and put into prison. Injunctions are commonly used against such tort as noise nuisance or trespass to the person, which involves assault and battery and false imprisonment.

There are three main types of injunction available to the court.

- **A prohibitory injunction** is an order not to do something. For instance the court may order a builder not to cut down some important trees because of protected wildlife living there.

- **A mandatory injunction** is an order to do something. This might be an order to take down an extension to a house which is blocking a neighbour's access.

● **An interlocutory injunction** is an order to stop something happening before the case is heard in court, for example, preventing a local authority commencing building work on a public area.

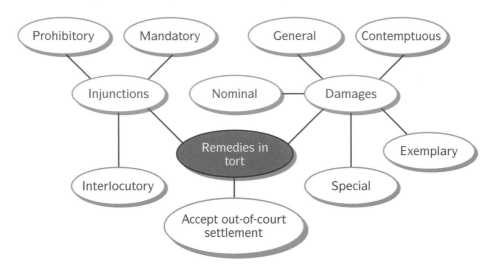

Remedies in tort

Revision checklist

1 Three elements have to be present for negligence: duty of care, breach of duty of care and damage caused to the claimant.

2 The objective test uses the 'reasonable man' and the degree of care he would use.

3 Judges also look to other factors: degree of risk, seriousness of the potential harm, cost of precaution, and the importance of risky activity.

4 The claimant must prove breach of duty has occurred. Sometimes *res ipsa loquitor*, which means 'let the facts speak for themselves', is used.

5 *Nettleship v Weston (1971)* meant that learners would be treated as qualified persons.

6 Professionals should have a degree of skill that matches the skill of a competent person in that profession.

7 Damage must be caused to the claimant by the defendant. The 'but for' test is used.

8 Problems for claimants arise when there has been a break in the chain of events, there is more than one possible cause of damage or it is difficult to prove that the defendant should have foreseen events.

9 Damages are one remedy for negligent behaviour. They include: general damages, special damages, contemptuous damages, nominal damages and exemplary damages.

10 Injunctions are another remedy for negligence. They include prohibitory injunctions, mandatory injunctions and interlocutory injunctions.

Quick revision questions

1 What three elements have to be present to prove a tort of negligence?

2 Describe an objective test.

3 What degree of skill does a professional builder have to have?

4 What did the *Bolam v Friern Barnet Hospital (1957)* case involve?

5 What factors do courts take into account to give a broader context?

6 What does *res ipsa loquitor* mean?

7 How are learners viewed in the tort of negligence?

8 What was the difference between the rulings in *Rondel v Worsley (1969)* and *Hall v Simons (2000)*?

9 What is the 'but for' test?

10 What are the key remedies in tort?

Exam question

1 *a* How does a claimant prove duty of care and breach of duty of care? (15 marks)

   b What factors do the courts take into account to arrive at a fair decision for claimant and defendant? (15 marks)

Exam answer guide

1 *a* Duty of care involves three parts:

   ✓ Foresight: the defendant must have been able to see the possibility that damage would be caused due to their acts or omissions

   ✓ Proximity: there must be a sufficiently close relationship between the claimant and the defendant

   ✓ Is it fair to create a duty of care: consider people in public services such as police, doctors, nurses, firemen etc.

   b A breach of duty involves the defendant's behaviour falling below what is reasonably expected of them.

It is very important that you use cases from this unit to demonstrate the points raised in your essay.

   c The courts will consider a variety of factors to arrive at a just solution and remedy for both claimant and defendant. These might include:

   ✓ Use of the 'reasonable man' to determine what was expected

   ✓ The degree of risk the claimant was exposed to

   ✓ The seriousness of the potential harm

   ✓ Cost of the precaution

   ✓ Importance of the risky activity

   ✓ The position of learners.

Unit 8

Capacity in crime and in tort

Key points

1 Crime and children under the age of ten
2 Crime and children over the age of ten
3 Tort and children

Why do I need to know about capacity?

Capacity in criminal offences and tort is a controversial area. High-profile crimes have raised interest in this area of law, and the Government has recently been looking long and hard at young people and their involvement in crime. Questions will inevitably ask you to consider the moral issues involved in trying and sentencing young people and children in our justice system.

Crime and capacity

1   Crime and children under the age of ten

The term *capacity* refers to whether an individual can be:

- responsible for a criminal act: are they capable of forming the *mens rea* for the crime?

- held liable and be forced to pay compensation for an action involving the law of tort.

The **Children and Young Person's Act 1963** Section 16 states that no child under the age of ten can be found guilty of any offence. They cannot be held criminally responsible for their actions. The legal phrase used to describe this state of affairs is *doli incapax*.

Children are assumed incapable of forming a *mens rea* if they are under ten years old. The **Crime and Disorder Act 1998** has a provision covering those under ten if they commit acts which would have been offences if they were over ten. A Child Safety Order can be made which will give support to the child via Social Services and other agencies. It may involve the child being taken into local authority care.

Group activity

Discuss reasons for and against the principle of *doli incapax*. Do you agree that children under ten are incapable of forming *mens rea*? What would the consequences be if there were no age limit placed upon the supposed capacity to commit crime in young children?

2   Crime and children over the age of ten

The law changed with regard to children aged ten to thirteen with the **Crime and Disorder Act 1998**. Children over the age of ten are now treated the same as adults when it comes to the question of whether they are capable of crime. Children are now held fully responsible for their actions.

Child offenders and **young persons** are tried in the Youth Court. This court is part of the magistrates system, but it is different in some key respects. There is no public gallery, and no press reporters are allowed into court. The defendant is accompanied by a parent/guardian/responsible person. The procedures and nature of the court are less formal than in the main Magistrates' Court.

If an offender between ten and seventeen is charged with a very serious offence such as murder, they will be tried in the Crown Court. They may also appear in the Crown Court if they are a co-defendant with an adult defendant.

Legal case: T v UK V v UK (2000)

The murderers of toddler James Bulger, Robert Thompson and John Venables, appealed against the way their trial had been conducted. They used Article 6 of the European Convention on Human Rights, which demands a fair trial for all. They felt that the conduct and proceedings of the trial did not allow them to put their case fairly. They were ten years old at the time of the offence. Their sentences were reduced as a result of the appeal.

Jargon buster

Child offenders are classed as those between the ages of ten and thirteen. **Young persons** are classed as those between fourteen and seventeen. Above this age all are classed as adult offenders.

Group activity

Do you think the **Crime and Disorder Act 1998** treats children fairly? Should a ten-year-old child be considered responsible for their actions?

3 Tort and children

The law of tort involves the compensation for the doing of a 'wrong'. There are no clear legal reasons in tort to assume that children are not responsible for their actions. The only problem arises when we consider the two main aims of tort: compensation and deterrence.

Compensation poses a problem. If the aim is to put the claimant back to where they were before the incident, the defendant must compensate. Most children have little income and few assets. The phrase 'a man of straw' is sometimes used in civil law to refer to someone who has no assets. The prospect of compensation is minimal, so there would be little point in suing. This is precisely where most children stand.

Another possibility is taking the parents or guardians to court to claim compensation, but this has seldom happened. A successful outcome would only realistically happen when it could be proved that the parent or guardian acted irresponsibly with regard to the child and the incident. If the parent or guardian bought an air-rifle and allowed the child to shoot it in the front garden at the passing traffic, damage caused to motorists or vehicles might reasonably be blamed on the grown-up and compensation sought.

Capacity?

Deterrence also poses a problem. Can tort of negligence be expected to change the behaviour of children and make them act in a safe and mature manner, taking all risks into account and attempting to minimize them? Although there is little in English law to give guidance, in Australia *McHale v Watson (1966)* stated that a child should be judged by the standard of an ordinary child of the same age. In effect, this is the concept of the 'reasonable child'. Adult behaviour cannot be expected from a child.

Mullin v Richards (1998) gives us an indication of the English courts' view on children.

 ## *Legal case:* Mullin v Richards (1998)

Two fifteen-year-old schoolgirls were having a sword fight with plastic rulers. A fragment of one the rulers blinded one of the girls. Initially the defendant was found guilty, but on appeal it was stated that the girl's age had to be taken into account. The appeal court's view indicated that a reasonable fifteen-year-old would not have appreciated the risk.

Revision checklist

1 The **Children and Young Person's Act 1963** Section 16 states that no child under the age of ten shall be held criminally responsible.

2 The Latin phrase *doli incapax* means that a child under ten years old is not responsible for their criminal actions.

3 Children under ten are assumed incapable of forming a *mens rea*.

4 The **Crime and Disorder Act 1998** allows actions against those under ten if they commit an offence. Action may involve a Child Safety Order.

5 The Youth Court deals with children (aged ten to thirteen) and young persons (aged fourteen to seventeen).

6 Youth Courts have procedures which are less formal than the Magistrates' Court.

7 Children are not normally seen as liable in tort cases.

8 Compensation and deterrence do not usually apply to children.

9 *McHale v Watson (1966)* was an Australian case which stated that children in legal cases should be compared to ordinary children of the same age.

10 The case *Mullin v Richards (1998)* ruled that the child's age should be taken into account during the case.

Quick revision questions

1 Which act refers to young people and their capacity to commit criminal offences?

2 What does the Latin phrase *doli incapax* mean?

3 What provision does the **Crime and Disorder Act 1998** make for children under ten who commit criminal offences?

4 What is the legal position of children over ten with regard to their capacity for criminal offences?

5 What is special about the Youth Court?

6 When does a child appear in the Crown Court?

7 What does Article 6 of the European Convention on Human Rights comment upon?

8 What are the two main aims of tort that probably do not relate to most children?

9 What did the Australian case *McHale v Watson (1966)* state?

10 What did the case *Mullin v Richards (1998)* underline?

1 *a* In what ways are children treated differently when they commit criminal offences? (10 marks)

b Outline the main problems when dealing with children in the criminal justice system. (20 marks)

Exam answer guide

1 *a* All those under the age of eighteen are tried in the Youth Court. This means a less formal atmosphere and a greater chance for them to give their side of the story. Children under ten are not viewed as capable of forming *mens rea,* therefore cannot be convicted of a criminal offence. A child under ten may be subject to a Child Safety Order which normally involves Social Services. Special arrangements are made if the child has to appear in the Crown Court. This normally happens if the offence is serious or the child is appearing as a co-defendant with an adult.

b Children are a special case. They need to be steered away from crime. Custodial sentences may be very traumatic and allow them to mix with older offenders. Article 6 of the European Convention on Human Rights demands a fair trial for all. Children may be overwhelmed by the trial process and not feel confident in expressing their case. An awkward question is the age of capacity. Is ten too young for criminal responsibility? Give a reasoned opinion.

Acts of Parliament

Abortion Act 1967

Access to Justice Act 1999

Act of Settlement 1700

Arbitration Act 1996

Attachment of Earnings Act 1971

Bail (Amendment) Act 1993

Bail Act 1976

Channel Tunnel Act 1986

Children and Young Person's Act 1963

Civil Procedures Rules 1999

Contempt of Court Act 1981

Court and Legal Services Act 1990

Courts Acts 1971

Crime (Sentences) Act 1997

Crime and Disorder Act 1998

Criminal Damage Act 1971

Criminal Justice Act 1982

Criminal Justice Act 1988

Criminal Justice Act 1993

Dangerous Drugs Act 1965

Emergency Powers Act 1920

European Communities Act 1972

Finance Act 1976

Health and Safety at Work Act 1974

Human Rights Act 1998

Interpretation Act 1978

Magistrates Courts Act 1980

Mental Health Act 1983

Merchant Shipping Act 1988

Murder (abolition of death penalty) Act 1965

Offences Against the Person Act 1861

Parliament Act 1911

Parliament Act 1949

Police and Criminal Evidence Act 1984

Powers of Criminal Courts (Sentencing) Act 2000

Practice Statement 1966

Prosecution of Offences Act 1985

Race Relations Act 1976

Royal Assent Act 1961
Social Security Act 1984
Theft Act 1968
Trade Descriptions Act 1968

Legal cases

Anns v Merton LBC (1977)

B v DPP (2000)

Barnett v Chelsea and Kensington Hospital Management Committee (1969)

Bolam v Friern Barnet Hospital (1957)

Bolton v Stone (1951)

Byrne v Boadle (1863)

Callow v Tillstone (1900)

Carparo Industries v Dickman (1990)

Carslogie Steamship Co Ltd v Royal Norwegian Government (1952)

Daniels v White (1938)

Donoghue v Stevenson (1932)

DPP v K (a minor) (1990)

Factortame Ltd v Secretary of State (1989)

Fagan v Metropolitan Police Commissioner (1968)

Hall v Simons (2000)

Heydon's Case (1584)

Hill v Baxter (1958)

Hill v Chief Constable of West Yorkshire Police (1988)

Hughes v Lord Advocate (1963)

Hyam v DPP (1974)

JJC (a minor) v Eisenhower (1983)

Latimer v AEC Ltd (1952)

Marshall v Osmand (1982)

McHale v Watson (1966)

MPC v Caldwell (1982)

Mullin v Richards (1998)

Nettleship v Weston (1971)

Overseas Tankship (UK) Ltd v Morts Dock & Engineering Co, the Wagon Mound (1961)

Paris v Stepney Borough Council (1951)

Pepper v Hart (1993)

Performance Cars Ltd v Abraham (1962)

Pharmaceutical Society of Great Britain v Storkwain (1986)

R v Allen (1872)

R v Blaue (1975)

R v Cheshire (1991)

R v Cunningham (1957)

R v Gibbons and Proctor (1918)

R v Hancock and Shankland (1986)

R v Hart (2002)

R v Larsonneur (1932)

Index

If you've liked this, you'll also like this!

A2 Law for AQA

Having used this book for AS Law you'll have seen how well it covers all the information you need for your course.

A2 Law for AQA is written by the same author and follows the same winning format as the AS book.

- It is AQA specific so it will cover only material relevant to your A2 course.

- Exam tips and practice questions are provided throughout will make sure you are fully prepared for the exam.

- Summary boxes, glossaries and exam questions help make studying easier.

Why not order a copy of *A2 Law for AQA* today?

You can contact us direct on:

    (**t**) *01865 888068*   (**f**) *01865 314029*

(**e**) *orders@heinemann.co.uk*   (**w**) *www.heinemann.co.uk*